CHOOSE WONDER OVER WORRY

CHOOSE WONDER OVER WORRY

MOVE BEYOND FEAR AND DOUBT
TO UNLOCK YOUR FULL POTENTIAL

Amber Rae

WEDNESDAY BOOKS
NEW YORK

Printed in the United States of America. For information, address St. Martin's Press, 175 Fifth Avenue, New York, N.Y. 10010.

www.wednesdaybooks.com
www.stmartins.com

Designed by Anna Gorovoy

The Library of Congress Cataloging-in-Publication Data is available upon request.

ISBN 9781250175250 (hardcover)
ISBN 9781250175274 (ebook)

Our books may be purchased in bulk for promotional, educational, or business use. Please contact your local bookseller or the Macmillan Corporate and Premium Sales Department at 1-800-221-7945, extension 5442, or by email at MacmillanSpecialMarkets@macmillan.com.

First Edition: May 2018

10 9 8 7 6 5 4 3 2 1

For my mom, who ignited my sense of wonder,

and for my love, Farhad, who held a container for my light to shine

The WONDER Way

the journey to truth

CONTENTS

PART THREE: THE UNION

CHOOSE WONDER OVER WORRY

THE intro

aka let's get real

REAL TALK: THINGS ARE ABOUT TO GET WILDLY HONEST

As a writer, speaker, and artist, a question that I've struggled with tirelessly in speaking my truth—and a question that I became quite intimate with in writing this book—is "What will they think of me?"

What this question really means is "What if they reject and abandon me?"

As a ravenous consumer of vulnerable narratives, the stories that resonate with me most are the ones that reveal in vivid detail the journey of the author. Not the this-is-why-I-am-so-great-and-successful kind of vivid detail. But the this-is-how-I-fucked-everything-up-and-got-knocked-down-and-stood-back-up kind of vivid detail. For it's in their revelation of themselves that I can see myself more clearly.

I held myself to that same ethos in writing this book: to tell stories so truthfully and so transparently, and to fill them with wildly uncomfortable yet honest details that have me feel as if I am standing naked before you with nothing to hide. My hope in doing this is not so that you can know *me,* but rather so that you can see *you.*

This process of revelation—of turning myself inside out—is terrifying and invigorating and mortifying and exhilarating. It evokes my deep-seated fears of rejection, and strikes the chord of my darkest worry: that I may not be worthy of love and connection. Writing this book has taken every ounce of everything I have inside of me, and it's been a profound teacher for my commitment to living a life that is more strongly led by Wonder than Worry.

Every time I'm about to say something too risqué or too edgy or too truthful, the "good girl" and "people pleaser" inside of me screams, *You can't say that. They might judge you. You might let people down. Stopppp!!!!* There were many times in the process of writing this book when I questioned myself, the writing, and whether or not I "should" tell *this* or *that* story. It's then that I considered my two options:

1. Write the "safe book"—the one that won't ruffle any feathers or shake anything up.

2. Write the "true book"—the one that might ruffle some feathers and shake some shit up.

~~COMFORT~~

TRUTH

And because I'm committed to living a life that is true over one that is comfortable, I realized I had only one choice: to speak my wild truth.

My hope is that in reading this book, you will feel compelled to do the same.

Let's begin.

xo

Amber Rae

Don't die
with your
gifts still
inside

DON'T DIE WITH YOUR GIFTS STILL INSIDE

I was in the kitchen of my grandmother's house when the phone rang. "It's your dad," she said, turning to me and handing over the phone. "But please don't tell your mom," she whispered.

I was three years old.

"Hi, Daddy," I said. "Hi, sweetheart," he replied. "I miss you. I know I haven't been around much. I'm going to be gone for a little while. Know that no matter what—I'll always love you."

Even though I was only three, I remember the conversation like it was framed as a photograph in my mind. I can close my eyes and picture where I was standing in the kitchen, the coiled telephone wire I wrapped around my tiny fingers, and the way my grandmother looked at me when she said, "Don't tell your mom about this, okay?"

I knew something wasn't right here.

My father was a brilliant singer, songwriter, musician, and businessman. He was lead singer and played several instruments in a band called Dreamer. He used his financial savvy to give back to those in need. On his first date with my mom, he made quite the first impression when she tripped and almost fell into a puddle of mud wearing an all-white ensemble. Right before she made a splash, he swooped in to catch her. He had her, and every person he met, believe that the world revolved around them. When he was with you, he was *with* you.

But then he started running away. Between an abusive childhood and an addictive personality, the only way he knew how to handle his pain was through numbing. Cocaine. Rock and roll. Alcohol abuse. Cheating. Breaking into our home under the influence, taking me out from my crib, and driving eighty miles until my mom ferociously chased him down. You name it, he did it. He wasn't exactly winning at father of the year.

And then, just a few weeks after our chat, he took it too far.

Out for a bachelor party, and under the influence of who knows what, he decided to get behind the wheel. He fell asleep, drove off a highway overpass, and under a truck. The man in his passenger seat, who was getting married the next day, died instantly at the scene. My dad, who wasn't wearing a seat belt, was thrown to the backseat. He never regained full consciousness.

He spent the next year of his life in a coma, and the eight years after that with severe brain trauma in a care center. My momma, who wanted to protect me and the way I remembered him, kept me at a distance. That space dwindled when on a school field trip to a hospital in third grade, I asked, "Is my dad here?" I was curious to see the man who helped make me. I wanted to remember the way he would touch my hand and look at me. I wanted to remember being in his presence while he was still here. I was now nine years old, and Momma agreed to let me see him.

When we walked into his room at the care center, I saw a man I could hardly recognize. His face was swollen, and his mouth was connected to machines for breathing. An I.V. strung from his arm into bags of blood, and there were devices tracking his vitals. As I swallowed the harrowing scene I had walked into, my eyes opened widely when I noticed photos of me lining the walls at every age. My nose tickled as the sensation of tears began to well in my eyes.

I spent the next few hours with him, asking him questions he didn't have the capacity to answer, laughing at his goofy smile, and taking in the dose of Dad that I'd craved my entire youth. When it was time to go, I squeezed his hand and wished him well. I wondered if I'd ever see him again.

Every day after that, I thought of him and sent him peace. I wished for his misery to end, and for his life to begin anew. It was just a few days before Father's Day—on my grandmother's birthday—when I received the news that he had died. I remember that moment vividly—the way my hair was brushed up in a ponytail, the crossed position of my legs, and the white and flowered journal I was writing in—because in that moment, I felt the most profound sense of trust and relief. His suffering had gone on for too long, and now he could finally rest in peace.

What did upset me, however, was his wasted talent, creativity, and gifts. While I didn't have the language to interpret my emotions at the time, now I can put words to the wondering I felt as a kid: I wondered how his life may have been different if he had more direction, more encouragement, and more self-compassion. I wondered about the contributions he could have made in his one lifetime had he worked up the courage to face himself, to work through his demons, and to understand the root of his pain. I wondered what art may have come through him, what business contributions he may have made, and the sense of self he may have discovered along the way. He had so much to give, but he got lost along the way.

Call it intuition, my higher self, or a sliver of something I heard from Oprah once, but I very specifically heard a calm voice whisper these words: **Please don't die with your gifts still inside.**

And now, I turn to you, and say the same.

Please don't die with your gifts still inside.

Please don't be like the majority who regret what they could have done, but didn't do, as Australian nurse Bronnie Ware saw when she counseled the dying in their last days. "I wish I would have lived a life true to myself, not the life others expected of me" is what she uncovered as the most common regret. In their final breaths, most people hadn't honored even half of their dreams. Instead, they took those unexpressed gifts to the grave.

In the book *Die Empty,* Todd Henry says the most valuable land in the world is not Manhattan, or the oil fields of the Middle East, or the gold mines of South Africa. It's the graveyard. "In the graveyard are buried all of the unwritten novels, never-launched businesses, unreconciled relationships, and all of the other things that people thought, 'I'll get around to that tomorrow.' One day, however, their tomorrow ran out."

When I think back to the day of my dad's car accident, I can close my eyes and imagine the long list of tomorrows that may have gone through his mind when he decided to drive under the influence:

Tomorrow, I'll drink a little less.
Tomorrow, I'll make a more responsible decision.
Tomorrow, I'll watch my best friend get married.
Tomorrow, I'll call my baby girl.
Tomorrow, I'll resolve my differences with her mother.
Tomorrow, I'll finally record my album.
Tomorrow, I'll . . .

But his tomorrow never came.

I don't want to be like my father. I remember that thought so intensely as a teenager and young adult. *I don't want to be like my father,* which really meant, *I don't want to die with my gifts still inside.* It's only now, as an adult, that I can see how I was my father's gift, and his accident was one of mine.

His untimely death birthed me into the realization that life is fragile and every moment is an invitation to be alive. It led to my profound curiosity around what it means to live each day fully, which sent me on a path of asking—and seeking to answer—a central question: How do we express the fullness of who we are and what we have to give?

A CONFESSION: I WAS DYING WITH MY GIFTS STILL INSIDE

This book almost didn't get written.

I was too busy helping other people launch their books and careers, creating a global art movement, falling in love with an incredible man, holding personal discovery retreats around the world, sharing daily inspirations for a dedicated audience, and speaking onstage about creating the things we most long to create. Along the way, I realized I was very good at hiding from the one thing I most longed to create: this book.

I knew there was a message inside of me that I had to share, a truth that was ready to be expressed. But I kept getting in my own way.

When I got quiet and curious with myself, I peered inside and discovered a core belief gnawing at my soul and keeping me paralyzed. I noticed a conversation on repeat in my subconscious mind, encouraging me to do anything but what I most wanted. I discovered an all-pervasive, heart-wrenching whisper that crept into my dreams and waking life.

That voice said, “You aren’t good enough to do this.”

And let’s be honest, it wasn’t just one voice—it was a whole theater of critics that questioned my talents and self-worth.

I heard:

“Who are *you* to do this?”

“Hasn’t this already been done?”

“Will anyone care?”

“What if people judge you?”

“What if you get rejected, fail, and fall flat on your face?”

“What if you get bored? (You always get bored.)”

“Oh look: They’re better than you.”

“Your story doesn’t matter.”

“Are you sure you’re ready?”

“Do you have enough experience?”

And, of course, "Are you thin enough, smart enough, or talented enough to even do this?" (Ugh. *So annoying.*)

For many years, these worries ran the show. My team of inner critics ruled my life and kept me from writing this book for you. Years passed and little progress was made. Birthdays and new years would begin with bold declarations like, "This is the year I commit to finally writing the book my soul yearns to write!!"

I'd tell my friends. I'd write it on a Post-it note and put it on my mirror. I'd start every day with positive affirmations. Another Google doc entitled, *THE BOOK!!!* would be created, and I'd begin to write.

Then, a few weeks would pass, distractions would build, and suddenly all the other "important things" would take over. Slowly, I'd sabotage my biggest dream.

"Why can't I commit?" I'd ask myself, ashamed. "Why can't I follow through on the one thing that means the most to me?"

I'd watch with envy as friends brought their books into the world. I'd be happy for them, of course. *And,* my soul would ache watching someone else accomplishing a dream that's still swirling around inside of me.

It was a clear signal: You long to write. Your envy is a signal of the untapped potential within you. Now is the time. *Go, go, go!* The cycle of excitement would begin anew, but stop before I had the chance to be rejected or denied.

Maybe you can relate with something you care deeply about?

Is there a book you want to write?
. . . a revolution you want to start?
. . . a company you dream of creating?
. . . a part of yourself you want to discover?
. . . an idea you can't stop thinking about?
. . . a relationship you want to cultivate?

If you, like me, know there is something inside of you to express, and a kind of life you want to create, but you keep getting in your own way—I get it. I know your pain. I've been in your shoes.

That's why I've written this book for you.

THE CHOICE: MOVING FROM WORRY TO WONDER

Every child comes into this world with infinite curiosity and wonder for the world around them. Slowly, though, that wonder is socialized and conditioned out of us and replaced with worry.

It wasn't until I did everything I thought I was supposed to do and became who I thought everyone wanted me to be that I realized something was missing on the inside.

In an attempt to get back in touch with the curious and creative child I once knew but felt so far from, I turned my life into a living laboratory for uncovering who I am before the world told me who to be.

I began reading every book on self-discovery I could get my hands on. I met and learned with psychologists, healers, artists, neuroscientists, entrepreneurs, authors, astrologers, mystics, and leaders—many of whom you'll hear from in this book. Every day, I turned to one of my longest and dearest friends—my journal—to move beyond the critic and get in touch with the still, quiet voice within. I began exploring curiosities and ideas with a kind of wild abandon to see what felt right and true and *me*.

In the process, I discovered I was capable of far more than I ever imagined, particularly when I stopped listening to the critics inside my head. As I learned to look at every moment, challenge, and bullshit story in my mind through a lens of wonder, I ignited my imagination, opened up possibilities where they previously did not exist, saw the beauty and magic available in each moment, and peeled back the layers of conditioning to uncover and access the truth that resides within.

Each moment has provided me with clues and insights for my path, and now, for your journey with this book. Part master class, part memoir, part map—this book is a guide to moving through the myths that get in the way of being your most alive and actualized self.

I suspect you're reading this because there are aspects of yourself that you want to discover and express. I wrote this book to coax that out of you. To show what's possible when wonder leads the way.

Journal into Wonder

The answers are already within you. You'll find journal prompts throughout the book to connect you with your inner knowing and voice of truth. Begin with this inquiry: What is your relationship like with Worry? With Wonder?

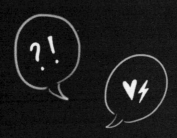

PART ONE

the TWO voices

MEET WORRY AND WONDER

Inside our minds there is a nasty little voice, a saboteur, a censor, and an eternal critic who creates a constant stream of scathing remarks that are usually disguised as The Truth. I call this voice **Worry**.

Worry says things like:

Who the hell are you to do this?

You're not actually going to say that, right?

Nope. Not you. Not ever. Not enough.

Look at them: they're better than you.

You suck. You suck. You suck.

You get the picture.

It took me a long while to realize that Worry's voice is not the truth, and is in fact *so very far* from the truth, that when listened to, will only take us further and further away from accessing and expressing the *real truth* that resides inside.

I finally stopped taking Worry so damn seriously when I learned to see it for what it is: a blocking device. A mechanism in our brains that's designed to keep us from doing anything too risky or too uncomfortable (aka things that are glorious and meaningful and worthwhile and life-altering). It was underneath my long and tedious tales of unworthiness, not-enoughness, perfectionism, shame, and who I thought I was "supposed to be" that I discovered another voice. A much more kind, compassionate, and curious one. One that wants us to do well, be seen, and pursue that which we most desire. One that knows with all of its knowing our truest truth. That voice is **Wonder**.

Wonder knows what we're capable of, and is committed to nudging us closer and closer to who we were before the world told us who to be. Wonder supports us in deciphering between the disempowering stories we inherited and made up, and the stories that strike the chord of resonance from within.

When Worry says, *Who the hell are you to do that?*, Wonder chimes in to say, ***If not you, then who?***

When Worry is on its high horse, declaring, *You're not actually going to say that, right?*, Wonder will ever so clearly state, ***You are***

here to speak your truth. Today. Tomorrow. Always. Is what you want to say a reflection of your truth?

And when Worry is inclined to keep the same soundtrack of judgment and fear and anxiety playing over and over and over again, Wonder will name the worry to tame it by saying, ***Hey judgment, I see you. Hey fear, I see you. Hey anxiety, I see you. I get that you're trying to keep us safe here, and I respect that. But we're on an important adventure, and you are forbidden from navigating.***

Worry and Wonder are perpetually pointing us away from or toward who we truly are and what we're here to give. In every moment of every day, we get to choose whom we listen to: Worry or Wonder.

Which will you choose?

Whenever I share this invitation with people, there is a resounding call for Wonder.

As important as it is to listen to Wonder, it can be useful to honor Worry, too. Why? *Because not all Worry is destructive.*

NOT *ALL* WORRY IS DESTRUCTIVE.
IT *CAN* BE USEFUL.

Last year, when I finished a talk about Worry and Wonder, a woman approached me near the stage and said, "My dad always told me that ninety percent of what I worried about wouldn't happen. I told him that's because I worried about it and figured out a solution."

We both laughed.

And therein lies an important point: Not *all* Worry is destructive. Worry *can* be useful. Sometimes.

Our Worry voice can express itself in two ways: as toxic worry or as useful worry.

Toxic worry is the relentless, looping thoughts that paralyze and prevent you from taking action or moving forward. It's the gripping rumination on the past and anxiety about the future—a habit that Stanford neurosurgeon Dr. James Doty said we spend nearly 80 percent of our time and attention on.

Useful worry is the foresight to imagine setbacks and challenges, make a plan, and take action. Worry is useful *only* when it's within our control and empowers us to act. So when our Worry voice chimes in, we can ask two questions:

1. Is this a real possibility?
2. Is there any productive action I can take right now?

When it's not a real possibility and there aren't productive steps to take, we know we're triggering what neuroscientists call the "threat detection system" in our brain. Thanks to evolution, worry and fear have been wired in our systems for millions of years as a mechanism to keep us safe. To some extent, we need it. Without it, your ancestors would have been eaten by saber-toothed tigers. You would jump off an outrageously high cliff just to see if you could make the landing. You would enter into a business partnership with someone who stated from the outset, "I'm entering into this arrangement with the intention of using you and taking your money." You would fall in love with someone who said, "I have no desire of ever committing to you."

Worry prevents us from actual threats to our survival, like the ones I've listed above. But when it comes to pursuing what's meaningful to us, those desires typically come along with some level of uncertainty and unknown, which our brains label as "dangerous." That's when Worry starts screaming for safety, and we're inclined to shut down, avoid new experiences, seek familiarity, and push away our dreams. When this happens—when the experience of worry isn't bringing us closer to who we are and the gifts we're here to give—it's noise. A toxic and paralyzing ricocheting inside our minds that, if not monitored, can strangle the life out of us.

Toxic worry is the source of our unrealized potential and unfinished projects. It's why writers don't write, designers don't design, innovators don't innovate, and leaders don't lead. It's why we commit to making changes in our life, and then sit squarely in our zone of comfort. It's why we succumb to the mediocre directives of those who came before us, and commit to belief structures that leave us exhausted, resentful, angry, and drained. It's why the things we long for most—the ideas we can't stop thinking about, the rituals we want to cultivate, and the lives we want to create—stay unrealized in our hearts, masked by fear and doubt.

The lengths to which we'll go to avoid what we long for is what Steven Pressfield refers to as "Resistance" in his book *The War of Art*. "Most of us have two lives," he says. "The life we live, and the unlived life within us. Between the two stands Resistance."

In perhaps one of my favorite and most eye-opening excerpts, Pressfield says, "You know, Hitler wanted to be an artist. At eighteen he took his inheritance, seven hundred kronen, and moved to Vienna to live and study. He applied to the Academy of Fine Arts and later to the School of Architecture. Ever see one of his paintings? Neither have I. Resistance beat him. Call it overstatement but I'll say it anyway: it was easier for Hitler to start World War II than it was for him to face a blank square of canvas."

Not facing ourselves—and our demons—is what keeps our greatest lives locked away inside. So, knowing that the toxic voice of Worry that speaks with criticism and disapproval is stifling us, why don't we listen to Wonder? Why don't we trust the voice of curiosity, compassion, and love? Why don't we go after the things we say we want most?

Here's why:

THE MYTH OF "NOT ENOUGH"

Beneath our unfinished projects, unrealized dreams, and unexpressed truths lies a central myth that gnaws at us more deeply than any other. I saw this myth kill my father, I've experienced it strangle my gifts, and I've witnessed it suck the creativity, talent, and potential out of the many thousands of people I've worked with over the years.

That myth is this: *I am not enough.*

I am not smart enough.

I am not talented enough.

I am not attractive enough.

I am not powerful enough.

I am not strong enough.

I am not thin enough.

I am not lovable enough.

I am not perfect enough.

I don't have enough time.

I don't have enough money.

I am not enough.

Sound familiar?

Journal into Wonder

Circle the myths above that strike a chord of resonance from within, and add your own. Then, in a journal, write about a time when the myth of "not enough" held you back, and another time when you moved through it.

I've struggled tirelessly with this very myth in my own life, and once believed with all of my being that I was the only person being strangled by this fear. I couldn't have been more wrong.

This very belief of "not enough" is what I've found at the core of the suffering of every single creative, entrepreneur, leader, and evolving human—as well as those who aspire to be. I've worked with creatives who came into this world through profound abuse or extreme poverty and thus carry a deep-seated fear of being unwanted and inadequate. I've advised leaders who have hundreds of millions of dollars to their name, and yet still buy into the false illusion that they don't have enough time or money to realize their potential. And I've supported entrepreneurs who've had deeply encouraging and loving childhoods, and yet still find themselves trapped in a cycle of trying to prove that they are enough.

Despite the wide range of upbringings and circumstances, cultures and value systems, the prevailing and pervasive belief is always the same: *Not enough.*

At the core of our comparison, our numbing, our perfectionism, our paralysis, and our shame lies this myth of "not enough." It's the result of years of internal conditioning and deeply ingrained familial, cultural, societal, and religious beliefs. It's composed of how we were parented, the community and culture we were raised in, the media and information we consumed, and the stories we inherited and took on as our own. When we operate from the dominant myth of "not enough," it becomes the recurring Worry voice in our mind, and the lens through which we think, feel, and act. This shapes who we are and what we think we are capable of.

Setting ourselves free from this belief begins when we learn to see the stories in our mind for what they are: **myths, not truths.**

The myth of "not enough" existed long before we came into the world and it will likely persist long after we leave it. We do, as always, have a choice. We can buy into the myth and let it run our lives. Or, we can question it, and create a new story that lets us thrive.

And that, my friend, is how we Choose Wonder.

THE ART OF CHOOSING WONDER

As I once heard my favorite poet IN-Q say, "We will always find the evidence for what we choose to believe."

Beliefs and stories grip our lives in powerful ways. Something happens, we draw meaning from it, and that interpretation impacts how we feel and what we choose to believe about ourselves and the world. Sometimes these stories serve us. Other times, they hold us back. Much of the fear, anxiety, and stress that we experience in everyday life is self-created based on what we're choosing to tell ourselves.

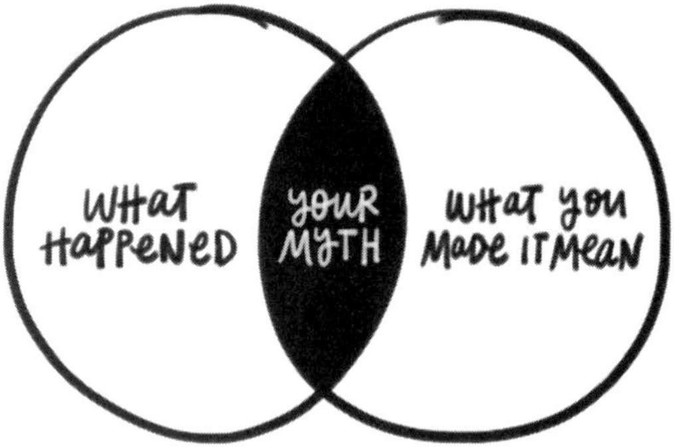

When I look back on my own life, and the times when I felt disconnected from myself and my gifts, it's because my mind was running wild with unexamined myths. Whether I was popping Adderall to be thin because then I thought "men would love me," or playing small because I told myself "I'm not worthy to be here," or holding back my truth because I believed a mentor when he said, "Your story doesn't matter," these beliefs prevented me from living from a place of my fullest self-expression. As I learned from author and teacher Byron Katie, "When I believed my thoughts, I suffered, but when I didn't believe them, I didn't suffer, and this is true for every human being. Freedom is as simple as that."

Journal into Wonder

Think of a reoccurring worry voice that's stifling you. Then, try using Byron Katie's four questions from her method of self-inquiry called The Work: 1. Is it true? (If no, move to 3.) 2. Can you absolutely know that it's true? 3. How do you react, what happens, when you believe that thought? 4. Who would you be without the thought?

How we undo these stories—and rise above them—is by turning toward the discomfort, rather than trying to push it away. It's noticing the stories we tell ourselves that cause us pain, and then asking: 1) where did this belief come from? and 2) what is it revealing about my growth? That's the art of Choosing Wonder.

When I first began getting in touch with my myths of unworthiness, shame, and not-good-enoughness, it took me quite some time to realize that my uncomfortable feelings were not my foes. My inclination was to try to overcome, get rid of, or make the discomfort go away. I thought that if I placed the-time-my-heart-shattered-into-a-million-pieces and the-grief-I-didn't-let-myself-feel and the-betrayal-from-a-decade-ago into a box with a pretty bow, and then put it on the top shelf in my closet, the uncomfortable feelings would magically disappear. I was alarmed, years later, to discover that not only did they not go away, they had increased in size.

With an affinity toward being positive, making the most of each moment, and finding the silver lining in all situations, I discovered that I was missing out on the growth, wisdom, and light that come along with entering the darker places. As I moved toward the struggle, I moved toward the light.

It was only when I learned to turn toward and honor my inner ache—and get curious about what it was trying to tell me—that I was able to access and unlock a deeper love, kindness, and joy within. It wasn't my feelings that were the problem, I discovered. It was my relationship *to them*.

In a workshop with bestselling memoirist Cheryl Strayed, she said, "We all have an invisible terrible someone, and we must find a way to work with these people." Rather than try to "kill them off," she likens her approach to talking to them over wine. I too like to imagine clinking a glass of Pinot Noir with my Worry voices. After we swirl our glasses and take a sip, I lean forward, and say, "Hey you—I'm here for you. What is it that you want me to know?" This invitation allows me to take the mask off the "enemy" that seems oh-so-scary and uncover an ally that I have the chance to get to know.

Our Feelings aren't the problem. It's our relationship to them.

Journal into Wonder

Bring to mind a voice inside your head that's creating stress. At the top of your journal write, "Hey, voice that says ______________, I'm here for you. What is it that you want me to know?"

And that's precisely what we're going to explore in the next section, The Worry Myths. As we turn toward our voices of fear, shame, envy, imposter syndrome, comparison, and perfectionism, we're moving in the direction of joy, beauty, magic, flow, love, and wonder. As we peel back the layers of our conditioning to connect with our truest truth, there are the three C's—Courage, Curiosity, and Compassion—who are here to be our guides. I like to think of them as Wonder's sidekicks.

THE THREE C'S TO SEE YOURSELF MORE CLEARLY

1. **Courage**—Discomfort is a call to be courageous. Courage is not the absence of discomfort; courage *requires* discomfort. Courage walks hand-in-hand with discomfort as we unravel our worry myths to discover who we truly are. Courage says, "This is messy. This is scary. I kind of don't want to go there.

But I'm going to go there anyway. I know it'll make me *more* me."

2. **Curiosity**—Curiosity is the art of noticing that we're feeling something—we're triggered, our emotional world is on fire, our body feels tense and tight, something is off-center—and then wondering how those feelings are connected to a belief or thought. Curiosity says, "What were you thinking about when you felt that? What story were you telling yourself? What was the trigger? Where does that belief come from?"

3. **Compassion**—Diving into the patterns that stifle us can feel uneasy at first. This is when self-compassion is key. Compassion says, "You are human. You are loved. I'm here for you—no matter what." We are all a product of generations of deep-seated stories, and we're all doing the best we know how based on our own level of awareness. Compassion reminds us to cultivate empathy for ourselves and others because we're all navigating our own damaging patterns of unworthiness, shame, guilt, resentment, and pain.

With courage, curiosity, and compassion by your side, every moment becomes an opportunity to see yourself more clearly. An invitation to step into the wholeness of who you are.

The WORRY Myths

PART TWO

"I'M DOING WHAT I THOUGHT I WAS 'SUPPOSED TO BE DOING.' AND I HATE IT." MEET SHOULD.

Every time I speak, I meet a number of women and men who, despite their very different circumstances, ask the very same thing:

Something feels missing from my life. I'm doing this thing that I don't really want to be doing but think I should be doing. It's not terrible and it has some benefits but really, when I'm honest with myself, I feel trapped, and scared, and stuck. There are all these people I'm afraid to hurt or upset, and that has me feel even more confused. What do I do, Amber?

I've struggled with this very question tirelessly in my own life, when I was living a perfectly good and comfortable life, and working at a perfectly good and comfortable job that I both loved and knew was not truly right for me.

There was nothing wrong with the work I was doing. I worked with incredible people that I respected and cherished. I worked with brands that others deemed to be "prestigious." The work inspired me and energized me and challenged me. People told me I was "lucky" and I was on a path to "great success." I enjoyed the work, though not fully. When I got really quiet and honest with myself, there was a very clear voice that cut through all the other voices that tried to convince me that this way of life was right for me. That voice said:

This is not your life. This is someone else's life. GO.

GO, because it's scary, you're afraid of disappointing others, and you can't yet imagine what's next.

GO, even though the prestige and success validate your ego, and you have no idea who you are yet.

GO, because the hunger you feel inside of you is stronger than any other hunger you've felt before.

GO, because that's what you truly, deeply, and wholeheartedly long for.

GO.

Every morning for nine months, I heard this same call.

Go to New York, my heart whispered. *Go.* I didn't know why I had to go to New York, but at the same time, *I knew.* There was an allure to the concrete jungle where dreams were made, the freedom the city so rightly embodied, and the eclectic cultures and ambitions that ran rampant through the streets. I could close my eyes and see myself there, hair blowing in the wind, energy rushing through me, eyes wide open to every new sight and sound. That vision enlivened me.

The only problem? I had an apartment of furniture in San Francisco, a car, a job in tech, and—in the eyes of friends and mentors—a very promising future. A future that, up until that moment, I thought I was *supposed to* have, and *supposed to* want. A future that, I felt guilty and ashamed, I *didn't* want.

There was a new me emerging, and I wanted to know her. The creative writing, psychology-and-philosophy reading, Pinot Noir drinking, self-discovering me. The me that wanted to love, and be loved. The me that wanted to put myself into situations that stretched me, just to see all the ways I could be stretched. And that *new me* felt so distant from the me I was trying to be for everyone else.

I had grown bored of the cycle of doing, doing, doing, and achieving, achieving, achieving, and I had grown tired of trying to keep up with the all the other high-achieving types who seemed to be having a ball burning themselves out.

What is this all for? I wondered.

When I tried to explain to mentors that I had this feeling inside of me that "I was living someone else's life," I received blank stares in response. When I sought counsel on my pull to move to New York, I was reminded of the career trajectory I was currently on, and how I should feel grateful. It seemed everyone had an opinion about how I ought to be living my life.

It took me many months to decipher my own voice from the very strong opinions of others. Mainly, the opinion that this call I felt was "the worst idea ever." It felt awkward and uncomfortable explaining that the only reason I wanted to make a drastic change in my life was because it "felt right." Making a change because it *felt right,* to nearly every person I spoke to, was not a well-thought-out or wise decision.

It was irrational. Impulsive. Irresponsible. I was too young to be making grand decisions about my life and career. I was naive and "living on my own planet." I was *selfish.*

Selfish. That's a loaded word that we love to throw around at people who choose themselves first. Who know and honor their own needs. "Selfish" is a word we love to project onto those who do something we're afraid we could never summon the courage to do:

Live out our wild truth, and pursue that which we long for most.

Pursuing what we long to do is not often celebrated and applauded. It's not encouraged or revered. And that's because it's unknown. Unorthodox. Mysterious. The mystery of what's possible tends to be hijacked by the risk of how it could all fall apart. So we close ourselves off, put a cork in the dream, and place a lid on our truth. We begin to live up to the false ideal of who we think we're supposed to be.

I learned the hard way that I cannot fake my life. Years of eating disorders, Adderall abuse, empty achievements, and half-hearted commitments to be who I thought others wanted me to be taught me that I cannot pretend to be someone who does not match up with who I ache to be. I cannot show up, and do the thing I don't want to do, over and over and over again, without cultivating resentment, anxiety, angst, and grief. Without feeling like I'm going to spin out of control and lose my mind. Because when I do this—when I try to live up to the mirage of someone else's life—I am literally killing myself. Ever so slowly, and ever so surely.

It was in that tension between living out someone else's life and becoming who I longed to be that I had a chance encounter with a man named Amit Gupta.

And when I say "chance encounter," I mean: during my first trip to New York, over glasses of wine and eye-opening conversations, a sudden burst of inspiration struck. With the encouragement of the group, I grabbed a permanent marker, and wrote a poem on the bathroom wall of my new friend Michael's apartment, confessing my love to New York. He, humored by the full-length "art piece" that now graced his bathroom, took a picture and posted it online.

nyc—
the best coast
so much
better than most.
san fran-
cisco
please end
your disco.
you focus on
originality
rather—
who you want to be
please try
authenticity
and be
a real city
like nyc

with love,
@amber_rae

"Why is this girl so down on San Francisco?" Amit commented. "She's not down on San Francisco," Michael said. "She's high on New York. Why don't you show her the wonders of SF?"

And thus, a week later, when I was back in San Francisco, I sat front and center with Amit, a man I thought would be yet another person to convince me of why I should stay in my comfortable life.

"So, why New York?" he asked. And then it happened. That *Wonder* feeling. My longing, my pull, my inherent curiosity all culminated into a combination of words and sentences that seemed to flow from the core of me. Amit listened carefully, grinning and nodding, and then said something I never expected him to say:

"Go. Leave tomorrow or the day after. Go."

I was stunned. I was so stunned that the moment remains imprinted on my mind, because when he said it, I recognized that not only was there finally a person in front of me encouraging me to act on the thing that I so desperately wanted, but all the reasons I was afraid to leave were now more evident and obvious than ever before.

"But . . . I have a car, and an apartment of furniture," I said.

"Sell them."

"But I have a job."

"Quit."

"But I only have a thousand dollars in savings."

"That makes a better story."

I no longer had any excuses not to go. Because my wonder about what was possible was just ever so slightly stronger than my worry about how it might be a terribly irresponsible decision, I booked a flight. I wrote a resignation letter. I put my car and furniture up for sale. I freed myself by summoning the courage to separate myself from who I thought I *should* be.

Should, as author Elle Luna says, "is how other people want us to live our lives." Should lives in a world of right and wrong and good and bad. Should says, "There is only one option here: do it this way, *or else*." That's where "could" comes in. Could says, "Yeah, you *could* do it that way. You could also do it this other way. Which do you prefer?"

I suspect there might be a sliver of something inside of you that knows that you, too, cannot be anyone other than who you ache to be. You cannot live out the illusion of someone you are not. You cannot continue to live a life that is not *truly yours*. You cannot keep choosing a life of Should.

If there's something you've been waiting to do, or say, or become—or a curiosity you've been wanting to explore—I'm looking you in the eye the way Amit looked in mine, and I'm saying: *I see you. I get it. GO.*

GO, because it's scary, you're afraid of disappointing others, and you can't yet imagine what comes next.

GO, because the hunger you feel inside of you is stronger than any other hunger you've felt before.

GO, because that's what you truly, deeply, and wholeheartedly long for. GO.

It may not go as you plan, and it may push and challenge you in ways that you can't yet imagine. That's the point.

If you see every challenge as a gift in disguise, I promise you this: Your experiences will reveal to you the strength of your character, the extent of your courage, and the resilience of your spirit. You will burn down the stories you've been telling yourself about yourself, and emerge reborn. Every moment of "Oh shit" will lead to "Aha!"—and every trial and tribulation will show you what you're capable of.

The only questions that remain, then, are this: When will you do it? Will you keep putting off the journey of uncovering who you truly are? Or will you jump in now, and begin?

Your journey starts now. *BEGIN*.

Journal into Wonder

A tip I learned from psychologist Gay Hendricks: When you're wondering, "Should I stay or should I go?," tune in to an imaginary future, and ask, "Do I wish I'd left or stayed?" Notice your whole body's response. Do you feel light or do you feel tight? The light way is the right way.

The WONDERVENTION

① I SHOULD...

② DO I WANT TO?

③ I COULD INSTEAD...

④ MY NEXT MOVE IS...

YOUR LIFE, YOUR WAY

"I WANT__________, AND I'M AFRAID I'LL NEVER GET IT." MEET FEAR.

Of course we want to live out the truth of who we are. Of course we want to follow our curiosities, speak our truth, and pursue what's meaningful to us. And yet, the majority of the people who reach out to me ask about how they can do just that. Some are stuck in a "dead-end job" and searching for purpose. Some are at the top of their game and "feel like a fraud." Some are living their dream, but lack confidence and momentum. Some feel seriously broken because of a business or relationship or project falling apart, and they are quite convinced they'll never be able to find that sense of love and belonging and connection again. As unique as each person is, the central question of their inquiry is always the same: *I want ____________, and I'm afraid I'll never get it.*

I want to . . .

Follow my calling.
Experience true and lasting love.

Have the best sex of my life.
See every inch of the world.
Raise my kids to have a better life than me.
Use my voice.
Create wealth.
Know myself.
Launch a business.
Be in the best shape of my life.
Own my sexuality.
Touch this moment with my full presence.

You get the picture.

And then they ask for tools and exercises and approaches to overcome and get rid of their fear so they can finally go after the thing they want.

I get it. It took me a long time to realize that when I'm afraid, and when terror is pulsating through my veins, this is not a signal that something is wrong. Fear is not an enemy working against me, or a force that I need to go to war with and try to overcome. Fear has been wired in our systems for millions of years as a mechanism to keep us safe. The aim isn't to undo our response to fear or try to change it. It's to welcome it and learn how to have a relationship with it. It's to see fear as a reminder that we are alive.

So when you're frozen with fear, remember this:

1. It means you care.
2. You're on the verge of growth.

As a rule of thumb: The louder the voice in your head, the more you're moving toward something worthwhile. If you felt fully confident and comfortable, you wouldn't be stretching yourself and growing. You wouldn't be moving toward creating a life that reflects who you truly are.

There's a well-known piece of art by Jessica Hagy you may have seen on the internet. In the drawing, she expresses that outside your comfort zone is where the magic happens. I LOVE Jessica's work, and here's my version of it:

When I'm stepping outside my comfort zone, it doesn't feel very "magical." At least not at first. It's messy. Uncomfortable. Terrifying. The Worry voices in my head start going haywire and screaming for safety. It's when I second-guess myself, overthink everything, feel all the feels, and want to run the other way. It's why, after I started my own business, I kept looking for jobs. It's why a few pieces of harsh feedback caused me to put off pursuing a book for YEARS. It's why when I made a serious commitment in love, I freaked out.

When I first began stepping into the arena outside my comfort zone, I thought:

This can't be right. This is supposed to be where the magic happens. This is where I'm supposed to feel all the glorious feelings of fulfillment and expansion and bliss. This is where all the opportunities are supposed to come to me.

HA!

Eventually I realized that my anxiety, and the very loud and urgent Worry voice yelling "DANGER," is the very clear signal that I am leaving my comfort zone. The point is not to escape the discomfort, silence the fear, or make the feelings go away. It's to learn to feel them, see them, and move with them. And THAT is when the magic happens. The magic happens when we embrace and acknowledge all of our emotions, rather than try to push them away. The magic happens when we feel blindfolded and lost in the dark, and we're just curious enough to see what lies a few steps farther. And a few steps farther. And a few more.

The magic happens when we walk with fear—rather than flee from it—and see every moment of uncertainty and discomfort as an opportunity to explore the unconscious parts within us. As we learn to do this, the worthwhile vision tugging at our hearts will become real. Tangible. Out from inside of us and into the world. And isn't that the whole point? To express who we are and what we have to give?

Look, I don't have a crystal ball. I don't know if what you want will ever come to fruition. I can't know if you'll find true love and whether or not it will last. I cannot predict how the pursuit of what you long for will unfold, and whether it will be a massive and smashing success. I don't know if when you leave what has you stuck, and pursue what's next, it will provide you with the sense of contentment and connection you're looking for. I can't promise what will happen—if anything—when you use your voice.

But what I can tell you is this: **You are worthy of it and it is worthy of your pursuit.** Because your purpose and your call is to live. To follow what speaks to you. To experience the depth and breadth of what life has to offer, and what you have to offer it. To ask the questions that tug at your heart and let the pursuit of them be what you live for.

So, when fear shows up—which it always will whenever you're doing something novel and interesting and meaningful—and the Worry voice inside your head is saying, *I want ___________, and I'm afraid I'll never get it,* I invite you to ask a different question. A more wondrous one. One that will bring you closer to your truest truth. One that will narrow in on what actually matters in the long list of things-we-want-but-are-afraid-of-not-getting-in-this-one-lifetime. That question is: **What would you pursue if success or failure didn't matter?**

Because, really, that's the thing worth pursuing. The thing you'll show up for and nurture and devote yourself to no matter what. Even if it's not a massive success. Even if it doesn't give you worldwide applause. Even if it doesn't validate you in the ways you want to be validated. Even when it comes along with rejection and failure and missteps (aka meaningful learning and growth). Even if the only outcome that ever comes of it is joy in your heart.

When you take success and failure and winning and losing out of the picture, that's when you connect to your voice of truth. That's when you hear the call that can only speak to you, and through you. That's when you *Choose Wonder.*

IF SUCCESS & FAILURE DIDN'T MATTER, I WOULD:

CHART YOUR COURSE

"CAN I REALLY TRUST MYSELF?" MEET SELF-DOUBT.

Every time I consider the question, "Can I really trust myself?," a quote I love by psychologist Gay Hendricks comes to mind. He says that we will learn our lessons with "the tickle of a feather or the whomp of a sledgehammer, depending on how open we are to learning the particular lesson. Getting stubborn and defensive invites the sledgehammer; getting open and curious invites the feather."

One way of learning to trust ourselves is by noticing the times when the sledgehammer cracked our life right open because *we didn't listen.*

I have a friend I'll call Diana. For several months, she awoke at 4:00 A.M. in panic. She felt the same urge: *You need to leave!* She lived in an apartment, and a city, where she no longer felt like she belonged. She wanted to leave, but she doubted her intuition.

She wanted to go elsewhere, but didn't know where to go. *You need to leave!* she heard repeatedly.

But she stayed. She gripped to staying so tightly that not only did she stay put, but when the building she lived in went up for sale, she decided she was going to buy it. She put the paperwork together, and made an offer way above the asking price to ensure she would get it. And get it she did.

When the city came to inspect the building, peculiar things started happening. Workers told her they couldn't believe the building was still intact. Real estate agents told her the building was worth far less than her offer. People from the city came and put a giant DANGER sign on the side of the building because they feared it would fall apart. And fall apart it did. When a construction team came to fix what was broken, the walls fell down, the building crumbled, and all her things were destroyed. The deal she so tightly clung to vanished.

That is what it looks like *not* to listen. That is how you know you're not acting on what's true for you. It's a lesson that I too have learned over and over again.

When I first started working with individuals to make the changes they wanted to make in their lives, it went better than I could have ever expected. One man left the fast-paced world of finance, where he repressed his sexuality, and came out. One woman got a raise, began working on her terms, and started her own company. Another began writing and expressing her thoughts in a way that brought light to her past pain and trauma, which led her to move from the world of consulting into freelance writing.

As I worked with more and more clients, and as I watched them shift and transform before my eyes, I gained confidence. I began earning a great living. I felt a sense of meaning in the work I was doing. The word spread, and I had hundreds of people applying to work with me. It felt as if Wonder was so clearly guiding me in the direction of a path that felt true and aligned for me.

And then, because things were going *so well,* I freaked out. I began creating a stream of anxious thoughts to bring me back down to where I was more comfortable: not feeling so good. I began to worry my flow of clients wouldn't be sustainable. I worried I'd never make enough money to sustain my lifestyle. I worried the results were just a fluke, and I was surely a fraud. Gay Hendricks calls these self-imposed moments of debilitating and toxic worry "upper limiting." Each of us carries ingrained and unconscious ideas of just how happy and successful we can be. When life starts to feel *too* good—when we experience *too* much love or *too* much success or *too* much connection—we "upper limit" by manufacturing painful images of what could go wrong. It's a strategy for coming back to a more familiar place where we feel in control. When we're not aware we're upper limiting, it can lead us to make painful and destructive decisions that hold us back.

I certainly learned this the hard way.

Just as I was doubting myself, a very successful young entrepreneur with hundreds of millions of dollars in funding danced his way into my life with a shiny opportunity to make a bunch of money. Even though it was something I wasn't particularly interested in doing, I put my business on hold and jumped on board. I pushed aside the voice inside of me that said *Please don't do this—this isn't right for you* and I listened to the voice that said *This will offer you security and structure and stability—it's a responsible decision.*

It met my needs initially, and provided the cash and comfort I thought I was looking for. But as I continued to pour my heart and energy into a type of work that suffocated my soul, it led me to self-destruct. I began drinking every night to "take the edge off." I began eating away my dissatisfaction and despair. I stopped doing the things I was actually interesting in doing. I stopped talking to the people I loved and respected and trusted.

On one particular night, when I went out to a fancy dinner with the young entrepreneur who was now my boss, that self-destruction hit an all-time high. What started with a few too many glasses of wine ended with me getting into bed with him. This went on for months. Fancy and heartless dinners led to fancy and heartless sex, which led to fancy and heartless work and a fancy and heartless way of life. Fancy and heartless led me to gain thirty pounds in three months and begin breaking out in rashes all over my chest. Fancy and heartless led me to shut out friends who tapped me on the shoulder and said, "Is everything okay here?" Fancy and heartless led me to keep sleeping with the boss even after he told me that while I met "most of his wife criteria, I was two checkpoints short," so it would never work out.

On one particular morning, fancy and heartless culminated in the sensation that my heart was beating out of my chest. When I was supposed to be in a meeting with my team, I found myself on the floor of my bedroom in the fetal position. My heart was racing. Tears were streaming down my face. My mind was spinning with so many thoughts of what-I-didn't-do-but-wish-I-would-have-done, and how-I-was-a-directionless-and-lost-piece-of-shit, and why-did-I-make-all-these-horrible-life-choices. My vision was blurring. My whole body was shaking. I thought I was dying. I thought I was having a heart attack. I thought this was the end. And when I thought this was the end, I was so pissed off that this was how it was ending. So I screamed and I sobbed and I resisted and I fought and I felt rage and pain and disgust and shame. And when I had finally felt all the feelings I was repressing, I let go. I surrendered. My hands and feet and head relaxed into the floor all at once. And when this happened, the most profound silence came over me. My panic shifted into stillness, and as clear as day, a voice inside me said: **You must always obey who you are.**

That is how *not* listening can play out. *That* is what a sledgehammer striking your insides open feels like. And *that* is the precise moment in which I learned I must listen to and trust myself.

I suspect there is a moment from your life when you too have not listened. When the fear and the doubt and the illusion of security clouded your better knowing. When that angst led you to do things and say things and act on things that you knew deep down were not truly right for you.

Why didn't you listen?
When did you first learn to do things that don't feel true for you?
What was the trigger for you to self-destruct?
What did you learn?
What would you like to do differently next time?

Journal into Wonder

Tune in to a time from your life when you betrayed yourself. What happened? Why didn't you listen? What did you learn?

Those are all the questions I began asking myself after I quit that soul-sucking job. Thinking deeply about where I felt out of integrity and what I would like my future self to do differently served as both an empowering and a corrective force. Getting curious rather than defensive allowed me to understand the larger patterns at play here.

I stopped sleeping with my boss. I stopped saying yes to work that made my insides want to crawl. I started noticing when I used food and alcohol to numb my pain. I became aware of when and how and why I leaned toward "security" and "stability" and "responsibility" because that's what I thought I was "supposed to do." I started learning how to make choices that reflected who I really am and what I truly longed for. And that's when I learned to trust myself. It didn't emerge from thin air. It emerged through I-fucked-it-up-so-many-times-I-want-to-cry-now. It came once I had been brought to my knees, and into the fetal position, when my heart could no longer take the heartlessness of it all.

It came when I bowed to my heart and said: **I will always obey you.**

So the next time you find yourself asking, "Can I really trust myself?," I invite you to ask a different question. A more curious one. One that realizes that what trusting yourself means is living out what you *already know* to be true. The only question that remains, then, is this: **What's true for you in this moment, and how will you live it out?**

And if right now you're thinking, "Well, I don't know what's true for me," and that uncertainty has you feeling anxious, I get it. We've *all* been there. As my dear friend Dhru Purohit once told me, "Not knowing doesn't mean you are confused. It just means you don't know. Confusion is: not knowing, but needing to know. The "needing" changes everything. The needing is where the anxiety and stress comes from."

So take a deep breath. Relax your shoulders. Stop trying to force clarity. Get quiet and allow the answers to come to you. This I promise you: they *will*. It's happened before, and it will certainly happen again. Trust that everything that makes you *you,* and lights *you* up, and wants *your* attention will be revealed to you when you take the time to slow down and listen. It's all inside of you. Your job is to coax it out.

Take a tip from a writer I met on my travels named Colleen. She was struggling to complete a big project, so she wrote a letter from her project to her. It gave her the clarity and boost of confidence she needed. It goes like this: *Dear (your name), It's Your Project. This is how to proceed . . .* And feel free to replace "your project" with life, a relationship, a conflict—or whatever is tugging at your heart.

NAME THREE TIMES YOU ACTED ON YOUR TRUTH & IT LED YOU TO LEARN & GROW...

1.

2.

3.

"I'M NOT READY YET." MEET PROCRASTINATION.

One way Worry paralyzes us is through the myth that "we're not ready yet." First we have to go climb that next hurdle and get *there* before finally committing to what we know is true in our heart.

I once worked with a bikini designer who, in five years, built a thriving brand that garnered the worldwide attention of *Vogue, Elle,* and well-known celebrities. But she did so at the expense of what she most wanted but didn't think she was ready for: illustrating children's books.

Another client—an aspiring author—had a knack for making articles go viral online, but when it came to packaging his big ideas into a book proposal, he ran the other way.

When this myth of "not being ready yet" grips our lives, we keep putting off what we truly want in exchange for what feels comfortable and safe and achievable.

I learned this quite intimately when I started being asked to speak and give talks. Even though I knew speaking was a call that I felt deeply drawn toward, for years I brushed off the opportunities that came my way.

No, I'm too busy.
No, I don't have time to write and memorize a talk right now.
No, I will not fly across the country to risk embarrassing myself in front of a group of people.
No.

Every time I said, "No, I'm too busy," what I was really saying was, "No, because I'm afraid."

With each "No," a wondrous whisper within me would plead, "Please say yes, please say yes, please say yes. Just once. Even if just to see what happens. Please?"

With my curiosity just slightly stronger than my fear, I decided I'd commit to the next request I received. That invitation came in the form of a Do Lectures talk in Costa Rica. Little did I know at the time, this commitment was about to turn my world upside down and inside out. First came the swirl of insecurities about being seen that I didn't even realize were beneath the surface. They showed up in the form of an inner monologue that sounded something like this:

What the hell did I just commit myself to? What do I have to say that's interesting? I don't have anything interesting to say. I'm going to get up there and they are going to stare at me and form opinions about me and quite possibly judge me. Oh god. And it's going to be filmed. Then it's going to go on that website for lots of people to see. What am I going to wear? What if I look fat in the video? This is awful. What was I thinking?!

This monologue inside my mind haunted me for days and weeks. When I'd pull out my giant pieces of paper and permanent markers, and start mapping the stories I wanted to tell, Worry would jump in to say, *Are you sure you want to say that? Are you sure you want to be seen that way? What if they judge you? You know your story doesn't matter, right?* Everywhere I went, the voice was there. Staring at me. Haunting me. Inviting me to write a long-winded and apologetic email to the organizer explaining why I would not be participating in the event.

When I texted my dearest Laura to tell her about the "worry tornado" inside my mind that was hijacking my creative process, she offered a perspective that I needed to be reminded of. She said:

Become one with the storm in your mind. Move with it. Lean into it. Listen to it. Use it as fuel.

So I did. Every time I felt the tension of Worry, instead of viewing it as an enemy, I saw it as a signal that I was nearing exactly the kind of story I ached to tell: one that stretched me, challenged me, and had me feel seen. This perspective led me to the day of the talk when the winds were so strong that I thought I was going to blow over.

Dark fluffy clouds painted the sky gray and sat squarely above the outside venue that I'd soon be walking onto. As I sat in the audience, third in line, I repeated my lines over and over in my head. I placed my hands on my legs, trying to act cool and calm and collected even though I felt like a storm was about to rage inside of me. And when they introduced me onstage, the storm inside my mind became the storm pouring all around us. The rain was so intense and so loud that I considered running right off the stage. Instead, I repeated in my mind, "become one with the storm." I moved with it, allowing the energy of the wind to light a fire inside of me so intense that no rainstorm could extinguish it.

I gave the best talk I was capable of giving at the time. I talked about my dad dying and my failures and how to follow our inner calls and many of the things I felt afraid to reveal. And when I finished, the audience cheered as the rain roared all around us. As the raindrops washed away my hesitation about getting on that stage, I had a profound realization: **the very moment when we think we're not ready is precisely the moment that we are.**

Journal into Wonder

Where in your life do you not feel ready yet?
What small step can you take today?

When we learn to respect and move with the worry and the fear and the anxiety and the doubt, we're able to see it for what it is: **a signal of what we must do.**

There comes a point when no amount of planning, preparing, and predicting will provide you with the impetus and the know-how to take that next step. There are times when the only way to move through your limitations, insecurities, doubts, and fears is to do just that: to move. Yes, you have limits. Of course you have fears. This is true of any human, and especially those who choose to pursue something new. Those uncomfortable feelings mean one thing: you care.

Moving toward what you care about might look like that first stroke of paint, the first minute in meditation, or hitting publish on the article you keep putting off. It might look like setting a boundary, finally choosing to let go of the relationship that's destroying your emotional health, or moving on to undertake a big new challenge. It might look like choosing to give less power to the fabricated story in your mind about why you cannot or should not or aren't ready—just to see what happens.

"Let's just see what happens" became the rallying cry of the-love-of-my-life, Farhad. One of his earliest memories is running for shelter after hearing bombs explode and the defense siren that went along with it. When the violence and danger of his home country became too intense, he and his family fled the Iran-Iraq War when he was only four years old. By the time he was thirteen, he had lived in a refugee home in Syria, nearly lost his mom in an accident, illegally immigrated to the United States before becoming a lawful citizen, and moved nine times before landing in Palo Alto, California. While his mom nannied wealthy kids to keep the family's finances afloat, Farhad worked in Stanford University's food services, and slept on the floor of a remodeled garage they called "The Tiny Palace."

Farhad did not waste his energy and time feeling sorry for himself or comparing what he didn't have to what the children of millionaires in his surrounding neighborhood did. Did he compare himself? Of course. Did he question his worth? Indeed. Did he fear his future? Completely and utterly and exhaustively. Did he allow his insecurities and worries and doubts to prevent him from moving forward? Absolutely not.

Rather than be overcome by his fear, he moved with it by sneaking into lecture halls at Stanford, making friends with students and professors, and discovering how moved he was by entrepreneurship, innovation, and doing good. No one was there to hand him a manual on how to live well, express his gifts, and design the life he wanted. By facing and walking with his every insecurity and limitation, and by being curious about what could happen next, he created a momentum so strong that he was able to move beyond every obstacle that came his way.

You can too.

A few years ago, I sat in the front row at the United Nations to hear Oprah speak. (I actually took her seat by accident—but that's a different story.) She opened up to us, sharing that when she decided to start the OWN network after more than twenty-five years of *The Oprah Winfrey Show* being a number one success, she never anticipated the challenges she'd run into. When she found herself flustered, stressed, off track, and on the edge of breakdown—listening to what she calls "little person mind" (aka toxic Worry)—she couldn't hear herself clearly. The way she moved through the fog was to get still, and ask herself one question: "What is the right next move?" She asked and acted on that question until she moved out from the darkness and into the light.

Now I turn to you and ask the same:

What is your right next move?

Yes, you might be scared. Yes, you may have doubts and insecurities and fears. Yes, you may not feel ready yet. Those things will always be there, reminding you that you care.

What you're always left with is one question: What is your right next move?

Make that move. Start now. The moment you think you're not ready is precisely the moment that you are.

The WONDERVENTION

EVEN THOUGH I'M SCARED,
I'M READY TO...

MY NEXT MOVE IS...

YOU ARE AS READY AS YOU'LL EVER BE

"I DON'T HAVE ENOUGH TIME." MEET STRESSED THE FUCK OUT.

One of the biggest frustrations I hear from people is that there's too much to do, and there's not enough time. "Not enough time," of course, is a feeling. A myth. A story that when we buy into it, we run around trying to fit more and more into our schedules and lives. We rush from the next thing to the next thing, without appreciating where we are in this moment. We believe that if we do and accomplish and experience more, we will be happier and healthier and richer and wiser and loved by all. But instead, we're just stressed the fuck out.

Imagine that you're leaving for the most important trip of your life tonight. You're going for a month, and you're only bringing a carry-on suitcase with you. Inside that suitcase will be the clothes and accessories you feel great in, the toiletries you need, a book or two that inspires you, your computer and phone, and whatever else you deem important.

If you're like me when it comes to packing, you'll have the suitcase, and then a whole pile of things that you try to stuff into the suitcase. But it just won't zip. So you try a few things on to make sure you still feel good in them. You realize that you don't actually need four pairs of yoga pants. Maybe you even go item to item, as Japanese organizing master Marie Kondo suggests, and ask yourself, "Does this bring me joy?" You pick and choose your favorites, and you end up packing only what you really want and need and love.

That suitcase is your schedule and that most important trip is your life. And every time you try to fit too much into the suitcase, it won't zip. It won't budge. It's too full. Just like our day often is. Just like our life can feel. And then we wonder why we're so stressed out.

When I hear people say they don't have enough time, what I'm actually hearing is this: *I'm filling my life with so many things, and I haven't decided what is most important.*

I certainly know what that feels like. Before I committed to this book, I went to a workshop led by Elizabeth Gilbert and Rob Bell. It was appropriately timed because it was a moment in my life when I was trying to stuff that extra pile into my suitcase. And because I was trying to fit so much inside, I was kind of starting a podcast, and kind of creating a journal product, and kind of speaking all over the world, and kind of doing art installations, and kind of working with individuals and brands, and kind of writing—but only when I felt inspired. I was doing so many things and going so many places and making progress on it all. But I was doing it in a way that made me feel like my head was constantly spinning. Since I was skimming the surface of so many projects all at the same time, I wasn't experiencing the kind of depth that I wanted.

But I didn't know that when I arrived at the workshop. I was sitting there, hoping Liz could help me figure out how to do it all and do it well. That's when a woman in the audience asked, "How do you make time for everything that's important?"

Yeah! I thought. *How do I make time for it all?! Tell me your secret, Liz!*

That's when Liz told us about the time in her life when she was struggling to become a writer. She was working a few jobs, barely making ends meet, and rarely having the time and energy to write. When she shared her predicament with a wise older woman, that woman said, "What are you willing to give up, in order to have the life you keep saying that you want?"

Liz said, "You're right—I really need to start learning how to say no to things I don't want to do."

The wise woman corrected her: "No, it's much harder than that. You need to learn how to start saying no to things you DO want to do, with the recognition that you have only one life, and you don't have time and energy for everything."

You need to learn how to start saying no to things you DO want.

That sentence stamped itself in my heart and sent shivers down my spine. The words of the wise woman revealed to me what I knew to be so achingly true, but what I was having a hell of a hard time accepting: **I couldn't do it all.**

I had convinced myself that I *should* be able to do it all. I thought something might even be wrong with me because I couldn't. But that wasn't true. What was true was that I was stuffing so much stuff into my life, and I was making myself miserable. I no longer wanted to be miserable. I no longer wanted to halfheartedly do seventeen things. I wanted to will the one most important thing. So I went home, and I made two lists.

It's then that I recognized that there was only one thing that I wanted more than all the other things: this book in bookstores.

Journal into Wonder

Don't know what you want yet? Try these questions on: What am I curious about? Who's doing what I'd love to be doing? How might I turn my biggest challenges into a learning experiment?

So I started simplifying and letting go. I began karate chopping anything and everything from my life and schedule that did not bring me closer to this book being in bookstores. I said "No" to what I did want, like cocktails on Sundays, scrolling through Facebook to relax, and the other projects I previously mentioned that were not yet earning me a paycheck. This was not particularly easy. It was actually quite painful. But it was oh-so-liberating at the same time.

When we do this—when we remove unnecessary events and commitments and busywork and distractions that we think matter in the short term but don't actually matter in the long run—what happens is we stop acting like a slave to time. We stop blaming this construct called time for what is or is not going well in our lives, and we choose. We choose where to exert our focus and energy. We choose what to tend to. We choose the thing that matters more than all the other things. And when we do this, time begins to serve us, and what we're here to do.

The WONDERVENTION

① I WANT...	② I WANT MORE...
③ SO I CHOOSE...	④ AND WILL STOP...

WILL THE ONE THING

"I'M TORN." MEET UNCERTAINTY.

I hear it all the time: "I'm uncertain. I'm confused. I'm pulled in two directions. I'm *torn*."

Like with a man we'll call Will. Will was about to propose to his girlfriend because she was so ready to be engaged and he thought getting married was the next logical step. She was a great woman, and he loved her dearly, and after she dropped hints about them getting married for nearly a year, he bought a ring. He then planned an elaborate engagement which included a fancy trip and a fancy hotel and a fancy bottle of champagne. When her glass of champagne was being poured, he reached into his pocket to grab the ring box so he could get down on one knee and pop the question. But he didn't pop the question. He froze. He froze because in that instant the prospect of spending the rest of his life with this wonderful woman didn't feel right and true in his heart. Getting engaged seemed like what he was supposed to do. It seemed like the way to keep her happy.

"She's so great, and I love her, but I'm not convinced getting married to her is right for me. I'm *torn*," he said.

"Are you sure you're torn?" I said. "Is it possible that you're with a great woman and you love her but you do not want to marry her? Is it possible that having the conversation about not being sure you want to marry her—at least not right now, and maybe ever—is more terrifying to you than pretending everything is okay?"

Will confessed that he was, in fact, most afraid of hurting her. So he had the hard conversation. What that conversation revealed was that it wasn't just not right *for him*, it turned out it wasn't right *for her*, either. Her telling him that she wanted to marry him was her way of saying, "Do you really want to be in this relationship with me? Do you really care about me? Is this actually still working out?" When they got beneath all the stories they were telling themselves about why they should stay together, they realized neither of them actually wanted to be in it. So they broke it off, and ended up better for it.

I see this predicament unfold as it relates to our work and career as well. I once was sitting with a group of men and women who were part of one of the world's most well-respected incubator programs for ideas and movements. They were all feeling "stuck" in some aspect of their lives, and my role was to get them vulnerable and talking about what was really going on beneath the surface. We went around in a circle and pulled questions from a game I created called "Wonder Blocks." On the bottom of the wooden pieces were questions I had written like: "Where do you feel paralyzed in your life?," "What are you avoiding right now?," "What was your childhood like?," and "How are you *really* feeling?"

By the time we'd gotten halfway around the circle, half of the group was in tears as the real reasons for them being stuck emerged:

The only reason I'm doing this program is because it adds to my credibility and how other people perceive me.

I'm still trying to make Dad proud.

If I'm really honest—this is yet another way for me to prove I'm good enough.

The whole room hollered at that last one.

And then I'd watch as the light in their eyes turned on as they shared the thing they really wanted to be pursuing with their time. The kind of life they'd be creating if they weren't trying to make their parents proud and if they weren't trapped in guilt about the high expectations they felt placed on them. They'd describe in vivid detail what they'd be doing instead if they believed it was worthy enough to pursue. It was their voice of Wonder speaking loud and clear. And then I'd watch as the light in their eyes would fade as all the reasons for why they couldn't pursue what they truly wanted would come to mind.

The consensus was clear: *I don't know what to do. I'm torn.*

Whenever I hear *I don't know* or *I'm torn*—whether it's about the person you're choosing to spend your life with or the next step you take in your career—what I'm usually hearing is this: I do know what to do, and I'm not actually torn. I'm *terrified*.

Like Will was. Like half the people at the well-respected incubator program were.

If you can relate, and there's something you want but are terrified of pursuing, I get it. I've been there. Every meaningful thing I've ever explored was first layered with uncertainty and doubt and fear.

Before I left the corporate world, for example, I was convinced that my family and friends would denounce me. But they didn't. I made that up.

Before I applied to work with Seth Godin to start a publishing company with Amazon (an application that took me nearly seventeen hours), I almost didn't hit Submit.

Before I launched The Bold Academy, "a life accelerator program," my fear led me to delay the idea by working on other people's projects instead.

Before I called myself a writer and artist and creative, I hid behind other artists, and coached them to bring their ideas into the world instead.

Before I started The World We Want—a public art project that spread globally—I almost listened to the voice inside my head that said, "Who the hell are you to make art? You didn't go to art school."

Before I sat down to write this book, I was certain it was too late.

This is all terror talking. This is uncertainty and indecisiveness blocking the gifts that want to come through. When listened to, it can lead us to hold off, delay, and feel torn about what our next move is. To move beyond our fear, we must shine a light of awareness on whatever stories and beliefs are holding our lives hostage.

Because we're never torn. We're just not listening.

Our higher self is being hijacked by expectations we feel placed on us, people we're afraid of disappointing, resources we don't have but think we need, how it all might fall apart, and every other story we make up inside our head. The way to move forward is to let the monsters be seen and the scary voices be heard.

It's then we're left with one of two choices: to stay right where we are—torn and confused and afraid—or to rise above the myth we been living into.

I hope you'll choose to rise. I hope you'll *Choose Wonder.*

Here's an exercise to get started:

The WONDERVENTION

I'M AFRAID OF ______________________

BECAUSE:	MY FUTURE SELF SAYS:
1	1
2	2
3	3
4	4
5	5
6	6
7	7
8	8
9	9
10	10
11	11

Name IT TO Tame IT!

"WHY NOT ME?" MEET ENVY.

I recently received an email that went like this:

I'm going to be honest with you: My friends are making strides in their careers, and even though I want to be happy for them, I feel like I have a ticking time bomb inside of me that's about to explode. I'm constantly consumed by the question, "Why not me?" This eats away at me because I don't want to be the asshole friend who isn't happy for their friends, but when I watch them succeed, it reminds me of what I don't have and might never have. Have you ever dealt with this? How did you get through it?

Around the same time, I got an email from an illustrator that went like this:

I struggle with being completely open about how damn happy my creative journey makes me now that I'm following the right path, for fear of sounding like an arrogant prick. I notice that I put myself down so as not to make others envious but the reality is I'm mostly living my dream. How do you surround yourself with cheerleaders and how do you deal with people who envy you?

Oh can I relate to this. On *both* sides.

I once was the envious seething friend who struggled to be happy for others. When I witnessed others following through on the dreams that were still seeds inside of me, it brought up all kinds of demonic voices in my mind that told me I was not worthy or good enough or moving fast enough. Every morning when I jumped on social media, my story of being so far behind was reinforced by the highlights of others. While it was 9:00 A.M., and I was still in bed, blurry-eyed and yawning, my creative heroes were announcing the movie deal they just got for their book. A couple traveling the world had posted yet another video of their tanned toned bodies, and how they're making a killing in their careers, which made me want to punch them both in the face. My ex-boyfriend was now engaged and with his fiancée halfway across the world, which could only mean one thing:

I AM A TERRIBLE, AWFUL HUMAN BEING WHO IS NOT CAPABLE OF BIG THINGS. I WILL NEVER AMOUNT TO ANYTHING. I SUCK, I SUCK, I SUCK.

My feet hadn't even hit the floor and I was already raging into a bottomless hole of comparison and insecurity and doubt. I believed that because they had done it, there wasn't room for me to do it, too. I worried that I would forever live on the sidelines of my life, supporting others in launching their ideas into the spotlight, and I'd never gain the courage or the gumption to stand up and speak my truth. Then, I'd feel ashamed for the feelings I was feeling—*I'm such a mean and jealous human*—and I would retreat back into my hole of paralysis and fear and self-doubt.

Moving out of this hole required me to take a hard look at why I thought my success should happen overnight, and why the illusion even played out in my mind in the first place. What I discovered was that because my sense of self was so wrapped up in how people saw and perceived me, I was drawn to doing things that seemed "big" and "impressive." It's then, I thought, that my existence would be validated. The chirping voice of "Why not me?" was yet another way for me to say, "But will I ever be loved and applauded and chosen and esteemed?"

What came next was the difficult work of learning to love and applaud and choose myself. It was only through doing this that I finally learned how to cultivate a sense of *self*-esteem. And for me, that came when I showed up at the page, every single day. It came when I focused on the projects that lit me up, rather than where they would lead me. It came when I measured myself not against *them,* but instead, against where I was last week. It came when I learned to see my envy as inspiration of what's possible, and their success as a signal that there's room for us all. And when yet another person accomplished something that was still a seed inside of me, I learned to replace the Worry voice that said *You're behind* with *Just keep going,* and eventually *Why not me?* became *If they can do it, so can you.*

Just keep going turned into thousands of articles and essays and poetry, and dozens of experiments. It turned into a wholehearted love of the craft, a devotion to the process, and a desire to serve through my creativity. I stopped measuring my success by likes and page views, and learned to instead measure it by inner truths expressed. It became less about receiving validation and applause, and more about uncovering whatever in me was ready to come through.

When I did this, an interesting thing happened: The creative life I was once envious of became the creative life I was now living. And the more I acted on what was truly important to me, and the more I started making strides toward my right path, certain friends showed up for me like the old me. The envious me. The jealous me. The raging because I-can't-have-it-too me. I could see through their pretending to be happy for me. I could pick up on their inauthentic expressions of love and joy whenever I shared my good news. And when all I wanted was to see them succeed, and live out their fullest expression and highest unfolding, I recognized that they were still living in the mind-set that "If I can't have it, neither can you." I felt compassion for them, and the suffering that comes along with being stuck in that myth of scarcity—a stuckness I can remember with all my might.

A stuckness that reminds me of a story I once heard about crabs. It goes like this: If there is one crab in a bucket, it will climb out very quickly. But if there are two or more crabs, when one tries to climb out, the others will grab hold of it and pull it back down. I knew I didn't want to be the crab who got pulled back down. And I suspect that neither do you.

So to the illustrator who was afraid to be open about how damn happy her creative journey makes her now that she's following the right path for fear of sounding like an arrogant prick, and for those of you who shy away from shining too brightly, here's what I have to say about that:

Shine Your Damn Light

Please be happy about your journey. We need more people to be joyful about their paths, and living in alignment with what feels true for them.

When you are open about your enthusiasm, you will learn two things:

1. Who is truly and deeply an advocate for your success, and
2. Who is truly and deeply threatened by it, and who may even, consciously or unconsciously, try to bring you down.

It's not your responsibility to pull those who fall into the latter category up and out of the crab bucket. You need not be a savior to those who are still finding their way. Only they can do that.

Jealousy and comparison and envy can devour us, so please do not let how other people feel about you devour you too. I've yet to meet someone who hasn't dealt with some form of envy or comparison. The difference is: those who've moved beyond it were able to dismantle the scarcity-driven story in their mind that believed in a world of me versus them. In doing so, they got back to what mattered most: their work, their gifts, and the expression that wants to come through them.

And that's what's at stake right now: your best and brightest work. So shine your damn light, and let what you create radiate from the inside out. That's the best thing you can do for yourself, the world, and those who are ready to receive your work.

Protect Your Energy

You've done the hard work of putting yourself out there and acting on your ideas. Bravo! When you're doing your bravest work and on your right path, there will be times when you must protect your energy. Just when we start doing what we've always dreamed of, one of the ways we may self-sabotage is by turning toward the people who will bring us down.

Julia Cameron, a creativity teacher and author of *The Artist's Way,* calls this "The Test." Every time our life and career begin to take off, we may literally call up or seek out our most cynical and doubting friends. They, "for our own good," have quite the opinion they feel they must share with us. An opinion that is rarely for our own good, and usually for their own ego.

Save yourself the headache by getting really clear about who your true allies are, and who may try to bring you down. Get clear on what you will and will not tolerate, and hold that intention close. In other words: boundaries, boundaries, boundaries. Your very life and gifts may depend on it.

Journal into Wonder

Make a list of friends you can count on, and those you can't. Circle who you want to share your most important ideas and projects with.

Be All of You, Not Less

The point is this: be all of you, not less. You put in the work. You found a way to climb out of the crab bucket. Now it's time for your envious friends to do the same.

And if you're the envious friend who's asking, "Why not me?," my question for you is this: Will you climb out of the bucket or will you continue to allow your envy to devour you and the work that wants to come through you? I hope you'll agree: now is the time to start climbing.

While your envy may have convinced you that there isn't room for us all, I'm here to tell you that *there is*. Beneath your envy is a gold mine of wisdom asking for you to *listen*. Envy shows you what you want and are afraid you cannot have. Envy denotes what is oh-so-very important in a world of distraction and noise. Envy is a stream of inspiration waiting for you to grab hold and dive in. So start paying attention to your envy. See where it's pointing you. Listen to what it's trying to tell you. Let it be a call to action that shows you precisely where you must go.

Here's how to get going:

The WONDERVENTION

I'M ENVIOUS OF:	BECAUSE:	MY NEXT MOVE IS:

ENVY IS INSPIRATION IN DISGUISE

"I FEEL BEHIND." MEET COMPARISON.

I once worked with an artist I'll call Alejandra. When she reached out to me, she was paralyzed with fear about "feeling behind." She comes from an immigrant family and Mexican heritage. Her father values hard work and held the same job for over twenty-five years. Her mom ran the household, raised the kids, and took care of the family. Alejandra pursued a different path, and had dreams of becoming an international artist. She noticed these dreams coming into question every time she attended a large family wedding or gathering. Her anxiety and worry would hit an almost unbearable degree as aunts and grandmas and cousins celebrated and applauded conventional achievements.

As those close to her were getting married, being promoted in their careers, having kids, and saving for retirement, she was building her art portfolio, traveling the world, and connecting with like-minded people to help to elevate her career. At family events, she'd find herself powerless in a trap of comparison, where their progress meant she was behind. Even though she was creating momentum on her terms, she worried she was doing it all wrong.

I think of Alejandra as living on the spectrum of "coming alive" versus "getting ahead." When we focus on "getting ahead," we prioritize more, better, and faster. It's the conventional ladder-climbing, outcome-focused, do-whatever-it-takes mentality to success. Coming alive is different. It's recognizing that the path of "getting ahead," while perfectly suitable for some, is limiting *for you.* It's the awareness that the relentless pursuit of getting *there* can suck the joy, wonder, beauty, and delight out of the process of becoming. It's measuring how much you're learning and growing versus only assessing how much you're earning and achieving.

When we're in any community—be it friends, family, or a particular culture—and we're operating from different value systems, this can create tension that might sound like this:

"Have you found an eligible bachelor yet?"

"Have you started saving for retirement?"

"What is your five-year plan?"

For me, when I decided to quit my corporate job to start my own thing, this raised a lot of red flags for certain people close to me. "Do you have a real job?" was a question I received frequently, followed closely by, "How do you actually make money?"

GETTING AHEAD	COMING ALIVE
MORE, BETTER & FASTER	LEARNING & GROWING
COMPETITIVE	COLLABORATIVE
OUTCOME-ORIENTED	PROCESS-ORIENTED
DISCIPLINE & FORCE	ENTHUSIASM & PLAY
FOCUSED ON A "TO DO" LIST	FOCUSES ON A "TO BE" LIST

In the beginning, these questions put me on the defense, had me feel unsupported, and led me to worry that I was doing it all wrong. I ran from these questions as if I were being chased by a saber-toothed tiger, and avoided certain events where I thought I might not belong. And therein lies the key word: BELONGING.

Conversations that I thought were about success and achievement weren't actually about success and achievement at all. They were about belonging. Fitting in. Feeling accepted. For my family and friends who valued security, comfort, and "getting ahead," my focus on creativity, self-expression, and truth felt unsafe and risky for them. When they asked questions about my choices, this triggered my most primal fear of not belonging. Success and achievement just happened to be the associated subject matter.

When I realized I was dealing with a belonging fear, and not a success fear, I was able to reframe the situation in my mind. I first had to recognize that what I was looking for and needing was a feeling of acceptance. I wanted to be validated for the risks I was taking, the discomfort I was stepping into, and how I was challenging taboos and norms. This, I realized, was highly unlikely to come from those who valued getting ahead at all costs. Any attempt to prove my worthiness or enoughness to them was futile.

This is a pattern I've noticed among high-achieving friends. Relentless entrepreneurs who work day and night hoping their very traditional father will say, “I’m proud of you.” Creatives who are killing themselves and on the edge of burnout, when deep down they want someone special in their life to say, “You’re good enough and you’re doing enough. I love you.” When we look to have our need for belonging met through hustling for it, it can lead down dangerous paths. I had a friend who, for ten years, pushed himself to no end with his businesses. This led to substance abuse and multiple suicide attempts. On the other side of his healing journey, he realized that all he ever wanted was for the father who abandoned him to find him and say, “You matter to me.” *Not* feeling like he mattered was what led him down a path of disconnection and destruction. Learning to say “I matter to me” is what allowed him to persevere.

Moving beyond this pattern isn’t as simple as saying that we’ll no longer “need approval” from those we care about. We’re a social species, and we’re wired to need love and belonging to survive. What I’ve found helpful is disassociating feedback from being about *me,* or a reflection of what I’m doing “right” or “wrong.” Instead, it’s an opportunity to see into someone else’s worldview, and then to choose if that view is true for me.

So, if someone who has climbed the corporate ladder and is counting down the days to their retirement is giving me advice on how to live my life, I’m going to take it with a grain of salt. Or if someone who has yet to have a healthy relationship is offering me feedback on my predicament in love, I’ll be mindful of where their point of view is coming from. Before taking on what someone else advises as direction, I’ll wonder:

1. Do we have shared values?

2. Am I inspired by what they've overcome? Where they've been and where they see themselves going? Do I feel relatedness? Do I feel a connection with their soul?

3. What need are they looking to have met in sharing this advice with me? Do they want to be heard? Validated? Right? Respected? Are they looking to reduce their own anxiety? Or, are they sharing it from a place of love and wisdom?

4. Does their perspective and lens feel true for me? What resonates with me? What do I want to take with me? What do I want to let go of?

And as I do this, I've learned to calm the fuck down when someone suggests something that doesn't align with what feels true for me. I've learned to feel at home with my own choices—particularly when in the company of those who live differently from me. Because there is space for it all. Getting ahead. Coming alive. And every spectrum in between.

As don Miguel Ruiz says in *The Four Agreements,* "What others say and do is a projection of their own reality, their own dream. When you are immune to the opinions and actions of others, you won't be the victim of needless suffering."

So to Alejandra and to every person who's fallen into the trap of comparison, remember this: The only person you can measure yourself against is *yourself.* No two people have the same background, circumstances, desires, values, and gifts. When you're caught up in what *they're* doing and how far *they've* come, you're losing sight of what wants your focus and attention: your own right and true path. Trying to constantly be better can hinder your ability to simply be. What matters is where you were yesterday, last week, last month, last year, and the progress you've made since. That is how you get ahead, come alive, and achieve and belong in precisely the way only you know how.

The WONDERVENTION

CHART YOUR TOP 10 MOMENTS FROM THE LAST YEAR

"I HAVE SOMETHING TO PROVE." MEET HUSTLING FOR APPROVAL.

When I was in my I'm-not-good-enough-so-I-must-prove-I-am-enough stage of my twenties, I met a wise and wondrous seventy-six-year-old woman named Glenda. I was writing in a café about all the things in my life that I wanted to change but couldn't figure out how to change. When I looked up, I felt a sense of awe and delight rush through me as a bright-faced woman entered the room. She dazzled in a dress of blues and purples and greens and oranges that looked like a Picasso painting. On her face, she wore large round glasses with blue frames, and radiated with a smile I'll never forget.

I immediately felt pulled to know her, so when she walked by, I said, *Well, aren't you a sight! Is that a painting or a dress?!* She said, *Oh why, thank you! I made it. I used to be into grays and blacks, but that's when my life was oh so bleak. Now I only wear the colors of my personality!* As she spoke, she danced with her arms and her waist, and I could feel the life in her every word.

It seemed Glenda knew a thing or two about living so I asked if she wanted to join me for a cup of tea. *You know what, I'm early meeting my friend,* she said, as she pulled out the chair and sat down across from me. "I'm Glenda," she said—reaching out her hand. The connection was instant and it felt like we were long-lost friends finally catching up after years apart. We talked about love and art and magic; rejection and failure and fear. She told me about the screenplays she had written, the jewelry she had designed, the songs she had composed, and the men she had fallen in love with after the love of her life died. And then she said something so profound and so refreshing that I squeezed my eyes as tight as I could, as if by doing so, I'd take a picture of that moment and frame it somewhere in forever.

She said:

"In my twenties and thirties and even into my forties, I thought I had something to prove and someone I needed to be in order to be seen as enough. In my time, women were even more voiceless than they are today, so I pushed and pushed and pushed, trying to prove and show to all the men that I mattered. I went to law school and became a successful lawyer—even though I hated every second of it. I wanted to show my parents that I could and I was enough. And not just enough, but *better* than everyone else. I eventually became exhausted in that pursuit, and lost myself in the process of trying to play that game. I then realized that everything I had believed in my mind was an illusion, and I had made it up. I. had. made. it. up," she said slowly, while tilting back her head and laughing wildly. "There was never anyone to prove wrong. There was no game I needed to play. Other people were too busy caring about themselves and their own games to take too hard of a look at me anyway. So I ditched that old story, and vowed to spend the rest of my days doing only what felt like an act of love. If I couldn't do it wholeheartedly, I wouldn't do it at all. And look at me now!"

It felt as if Glenda was delivered to me in that moment to tell me exactly what I needed to hear. And perhaps now I'm delivering her words to you in the exact moment you need to hear them, too. So I'll say it again:

If it's not an act of love, is it worth it?

If you can't do it wholeheartedly, do you want to do it at all?

This is the hard-earned, I-messed-it-up-so-many-times truth of it: You don't have to do anything with half a heart. You don't have to play games if in playing that game you feel like you're pretending to be someone you're not. Pretending never works. Pretending kills your soul. Pretending is like a one-night stand on a drunken evening—going nowhere.

Invent and become whoever you want to be. Let the hours and days of your lifetime be one act of love after the next. No one is going to give you permission to write that edgy novel, to say "I love you" first, to stop doing the thing that you hate in exchange for the thing you love. Only you can do that.

So if proving has been the only game you've known how to play, let me ask you this: How's that working out for you? Might you want to try on acts of love instead?

The WONDERVENTION

By ______________________________,
(ACTION)

I'M TRYING TO PROVE THAT I'M

______________________________.

WHEN I DO PROVE MYSELF, I

WILL FEEL ______________________.
(EMOTION)

TO FEEL THAT WAY NOW, I CAN

INSTEAD ______________________.
(ACTION)

IF I HAD NOTHING TO PROVE, I

WOULD ______________________.
(THOUGHT OR ACTION)

MY HEART WANTS ME TO

REMEMBER TO ________________.
(INSIGHT)

BE ~~FASTER~~ ~~BETTER~~ ~~SMARTER~~ & ENOUGH

"I FAILED. NO, *I'M* A FAILURE." MEET SHAME.

There are the moments in our lives when we put our hearts on the line. We go after what we say we want. We pursue the call. And it blows up in our face.

I recall one such time when the shame was dizzying, and my stomach was clenched in a knot.

Through a combination of miscommunication and miscalculated risks, my cofounder Nathaniel and I had run out of cash midway through our first session of a thirty-day "life accelerator program" called The Bold Academy. Thirty thousand dollars short, to be exact. Our intention to bring people together to take their life and work to the next level instantly became clouded by the cold reality that we didn't know how we'd pay the twelve members of our team their final paychecks. The worst-case scenario in my mind was playing out right before my eyes.

Behind the scenes, Nathaniel and I were battling, trying to hear each other and find a solution. When I wasn't overwhelmed by the finances of the company, I was secretly navigating my growing romantic feelings for Nathaniel. Instead of leaning into the vulnerability of telling him that I was falling for him months prior, I chose to go into business with him instead. To top it off, I tried to convince myself that I wasn't *actually* in love with him by getting into bed with someone else. Now that new beau was an advisor on the project and member of the team.

It all came crashing down as we sat front and center with the team in my Boulder, Colorado, apartment to break the news. As I prepared to talk, my vision started to blur and I struggled to swallow as the Worry voices inside my mind started throwing a party: "You suck! You're a failure and you let everyone down! Something is wrong with you! Shame on you!"

As soon as I could catch my breath, I did my best to explain.

"We ran out of money. . . . We're doing our best to find a solution. . . . We're so sorry" was all I could muster at the time. The heat of my shame had reached such a boil that while my face appeared stoic as a stone to the team, my heart was shattering into smithereens. I didn't know how to express myself. I didn't know how to turn the explosion of feelings inside of me into a coherent narrative that would create camaraderie. I didn't know how to let them in, without destroying the "strength" I thought I was supposed to model as a leader.

Rather than turn toward them, I turned away. I was too ashamed by my actions to hear and hold space for their frustration and disbelief. Their anger and outrage only reinforced the story in my mind that "something was wrong with me."

So rather than apologize or own my mistakes, I hid. I played victim. I pointed fingers and blamed others. I tried to rationalize my poor decision making through the story that "this was a start-up, and the team should be thankful for even being involved." Rather than acknowledge how I hurt people—a reality that caused me *even more* shame and pain—I avoided it by sidestepping emotional discourse. Instead, I focused on the "logical" path forward: moving on, as quickly as possible. My avoidance led me to tarnish important relationships. It created chaos and confusion among the team. The family bond that made us so great in the start crashed, burned, and blew up into flames.

I was crushed.

The irony here is that all I wanted—and my intent in doing this work—was to feel and create a sense of love and belonging. But because I didn't have the tools to navigate my current of emotions and own up to the mistakes I made, I isolated myself and created separation.

I wish I could tell you that I picked up the right book at the right time, or met with the right mentor to guide me in moving through this painful period. I wish I could tell you that I had the courage to have the hard conversations—even if they were messy and heart shattering. I didn't.

I did do the right thing in some ways: I took out a personal loan to pay back the team within a month of the program ending. Six months later, and with a new team, we launched another version of the program—this time in San Francisco—which created enough revenue to pay off the thirty-thousand-dollar loan and break even on the whole project. We produced a powerful program that had immense impact on people's lives. Jobs were left. Callings were found. Businesses were launched. Millions of dollars were raised. Beautiful art was produced. Books were created. There were so many reasons to celebrate, but on the inside, I still felt crippled by shame, alone in feeling it, and unsure how to move forward.

I was exhausted. Depleted. So disconnected from myself. And I couldn't see the light at the end of the tunnel. So I did the only thing I knew how to do at the time: I quit.

I dissolved the business, labeling it, and myself, a failure. That label weighed heavily on my heart for four years until Brené Brown's research on shame came into my orbit. The research stopped me dead in my tracks and created a sensation of lightness and ease with each word I read.

"Shame is the fear of disconnection—it's the fear that something we've done or failed to do, an ideal that we've not lived up to, or a goal that we've not accomplished, makes us unworthy of connection," Brené says in her book *Daring Greatly*. "Shame is the intensely painful feeling or experience of believing that we are flawed and therefore unworthy of love and belonging."

Whoa.

The belief that I could be flawed and unworthy of love had been the story of my life. My lovability was so wrapped up in what I did or did not accomplish that I personalized my errors and made them mean something was wrong with *me*.

Not the business model. Not the decision making. Not the method of communication. Not the leadership style.

Me.

No wonder I ran/hid/numbed/fled the scene.

Maybe you can relate with a situation from your own life?

Journal into Wonder

When in your life have you made your errors and mistakes mean something is wrong with you?

It was Brené Brown's research on the difference between shame and guilt that really left me speechless. It's best understood as the difference between "I am bad" and "I did something bad." And the difference here is paramount because "we feel guilty when we hold up something we've done or failed to do against our values and find they don't match up. It's an uncomfortable feeling, but one that's helpful. The psychological discomfort is what motivates meaningful change. Guilt is just as powerful as shame, but its influence is positive, *while shame's is destructive.* It corrodes the very part of us that believes we can change and do better."

It's a feeling of shame that has us interpret our mistakes as *personal.* It's what has us believe that if we mess up or let someone down, something is wrong with *us.*

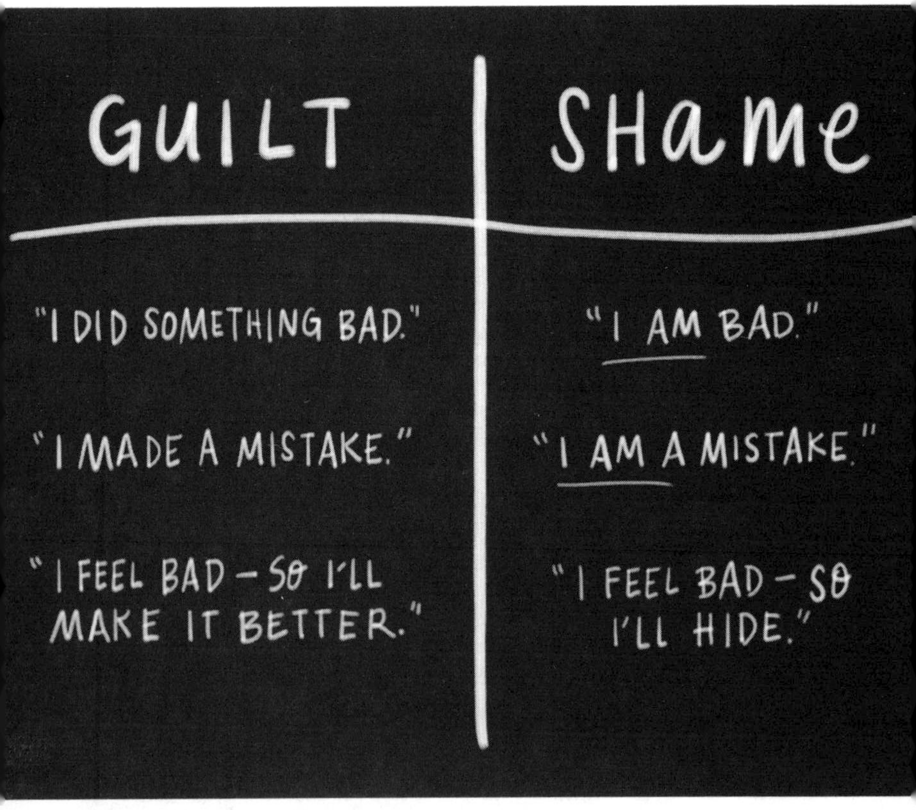

When I discovered this distinction, I wondered, *How do we rewrite this myth? How do we transform our relationship to shame?*

Brené calls this moving from "shame resistance" to "shame resilience," and it's a strategy for being able to move through the experience and come out the other side with more courage, compassion, and connection than we had going into it.

I experienced this firsthand, four years after The Bold Academy ended, when I finally sat down with Nathaniel to catch up. I remember going into our meeting with a sense of sadness in my heart because my-former-best-friend-and-big-crush had become a very distant stranger. I knew little about where he was at in life, what was stirring in his heart, and where he aspired to go. These were the kind of conversations we were having on a regular basis.

This time, I saw my sadness as an invitation. I remembered Brené's advice that shame is a "social concept," which means because it happens between people, it heals between people. While part of me was terrified that my letting Nathaniel in might create an even greater sense of disconnection, the other part of me was ready to lean into everything I had been learning about courage and wholehearted communication.

When we sat down on the black leather couch in my Brooklyn apartment, I opened a bottle of rosé and poured him a glass. I figured a little wine might uncork some unaddressed emotions. "I'm still really mad at you," Nathaniel said quickly. *Oh,* I thought.

This is good. He's letting me in. "Tell me more," I said, ready to go there with him.

"You really let me down that summer," he said. "What happened? What was going on for you?"

"Do you really want to know?" I asked.

"Yes," he said, firmly.

"Okay then," I said. And then the words started pouring out. I told him about how scared I was, and how dizzying the whole experience felt for me, and how ashamed I felt, and how much pain it had caused me over the years. I told him what I was most afraid to share, and what I had convinced myself that he had already known: my feelings for him. I told him how it was hard for me to see him with other women, and why I started dating someone else. I shared that I never told him my feelings because I didn't think he would love me back. By this point, his jaw was gaping wide. It occurred to me that he didn't, in fact, know about my true feelings.

I took a deep breath.

"I had no idea," he said, slowly. "I had no idea that's how you felt. Wow. It all makes sense now."

And then he shared his version of the story. We spent the rest of the evening going back and forth through the play-by-play of that crazy adventure called "Bold." The more we uncovered the wounds of the past—and the more empathy I felt coming from him—the more I felt myself heal. The more we got on the same page around what went really right and what went really wrong, the more I felt our bond restore. By the end of the evening, the "failure" of my past had become one of the most worthwhile and revelatory periods of my life. Sure, it felt as if I had walked into a fire and lit my whole body aflame, but more importantly, it showed me how to burn down my worry stories and rise through the ashes.

And so can you.

Journal into Wonder

Is there a conversation you've been avoiding because you feel ashamed? What do you want to say? When will you have it?

The profound lesson I learned is this: What we keep locked away inside will always haunt us, weigh us down, burn us, and hold us back. The way through is having the courage to pause, get curious, and own our story—first to ourselves. And then, since shame is a "social concept," when we share that story with the person who deserves to hear it, and we experience empathy and connection in the process, shame dissolves.

"I am bad" becomes "I made a mistake."

“I am a failure” becomes “I failed at that thing.”

“I am a terrible leader” becomes “I learned from my mistakes and got back up.”

“This defeat makes me unworthy of love and belonging” becomes “No matter what, I am always worthy.”

When we learn to stop seeing the experiences in our lives as a reflection of our unworthiness and not-enoughness, we’ll see them for what they truly are: a signal that we had the courage to get in the arena and give it our all. And now, like always, we get to do it again.

The WONDERVENTION

1. NAME IT

I FEEL ASHAMED THAT I ______ (ACTION YOU TOOK) BECAUSE I MAKE IT MEAN ______ (STORY).

2. TRUTH CHECK IT

MY EVIDENCE TO PROVE THIS IS TRUE IS...	MY EVIDENCE TO PROVE THIS IS NOT TRUE IS...

3. REVISE IT

A MORE EMPOWERING STORY IS...

OWN YOUR STORY TO REVISE IT

"AM I WORTHY OF LOVE?" MEET UNLOVABLE.

I vividly remember the moment when a man I was deeply and truly in love with—let's call him Jordan—told me he loved me for the first time.

As the words "I love you" came out of his mouth, my heart exploded with a kind of joy and elation that I can only describe as a sort of ecstasy. This man, for whom I was feeling the kind of I-am-so-completely-and-utterly-in-love-with-you-and-ready-to-go-all-in, was finally proclaiming to me that he, too, felt the same way. But then came the ten words I wasn't prepared for: "But I won't be able to tell you that again."

I was so mystified and bewildered and puzzled that he followed up telling me he loved me with his inability to ever express it again that the "I love you" fireworks died instantly. All I heard was "I won't be able to tell you that again," which in my mind meant, "I don't really love you."

I don't know why he said that he wouldn't be able to express his love to me again. I never asked. I was too scared it might mean something was wrong with or unlovable about me. I was too afraid that if I prodded for more details, he might turn away, shut down, and push me out. While I was busy taking it personally and making it about me, I missed out on the opportunity to turn toward him and say, "Tell me more. . . ."

I suspect now that his inability to tell me that he loved me had nothing to do with me and everything to do with how the word "love" came loaded for him with painful memories, profound expectations, and promises that could easily be broken. But I didn't know that then. His words "I won't be able to tell you that again" played like a metronome in my mind, keeping me synchronized to the beat of his drum and keeping me quiet to the beat of my own heart.

So I silenced my feelings. I acted like I didn't care. I went along nonchalantly with the twists and turns of our relationship, pretending it was totally cool and totally fine and I was so easygoing and down to earth about the fact that he could not express to me that he loved me. But it wasn't okay. It had me feeling crazy and desperate and incapable of understanding what I was actually feeling. Because I was living on his terms, and because I allowed his guidelines to dictate the way I gave and received love, I stopped knowing who I was and what I wanted.

I share this story because so many people write to me and ask for guidance on their relationships/life/career/calling, but underneath the veneer of their inquiry lies a question that nags more deeply than anything else:

Am I worthy of love? Will doing this make me feel loved and whole and complete?

People then share elaborate examples of how they sometimes feel crazy and desperate and incapable of understanding their own feelings and what they really want. Then they ask for guidance on why they feel the way they do and what I recommend they do next. Before we talk about where to go, let's first talk about how we got here.

When the terms of your life are created by someone else, and when you're going along with anything and everything that comes your way, and especially when you're pretending that it's all good when it's really not, that's a sure recipe for losing yourself. It's a sure way of forgetting where you truly belong: to yourself.

I learned how to belong to myself and create my own terms the hard way. After I chose to dance to Jordan's every whim for nine months, and smiled every time he did something that made me want to scream, he finally took me to a park where we sat across from each other at a concrete table. With a stone-cold look on his face, he said, "I want to be single," and I lost my goddamn mind. It's not that I didn't know this was coming—*I knew this was coming*—it's that I didn't know how to handle what came next.

Every feeling I never allowed myself to feel came rushing through me like a river. A faucet of tears streamed down my face, and whether it went on for minutes or hours, I couldn't tell you. The extent and depth and breadth of my repressed pain all exploded at once, and turned everything into a blur. "I want to be single" became "You are not worthy of love," and "This is over" became "Something is wrong with you."

The reason I was so vulnerable and fragile in that moment, and the reason my mind interpreted his words in such a deranged way, was because I did not belong to myself. I belonged to *him*. And because I belonged to him and not myself, I set out on a path to try to numb my feelings of not belonging with all the tequila, all the wine, all the attention, and all the career accolades. Every man I met and every opportunity at work became a game. It was a way for me to prove that I did in fact belong, and was undoubtedly worthy of love. The problem here, of course, is that I made up the game in my mind. There was never a game at all.

It took me a few years of shame and blame and pointing fingers and wallowing in my sorrows and repeating the same patterns over and over to finally realize in my pit of despair that I had work to do. This work required me to revisit the stories I had created about love and belonging, and where I had learned those stories from. It required me to get curious about why I allowed myself to be in an emotionally unavailable relationship that wasn't meeting my needs, and instead was tapping my insecurities. Namely, the insecurity that *I am not enough* so I'll take whatever I can get with Jordan.

What we had was not love. It was restraint. It wasn't I-am-becoming-my-best-self-with-you, and I-can-live-the-fullness-of-who-I-am-with-you. It was I-can-no-longer-recognize-the-woman-in-the-mirror kind of illusion dressed as love in a sexy suit.

And so I made a pact with myself.

First, I would forgive myself. I would forgive myself for the numbing and destructive ways I dealt with my pain and loss of power.

Second, I would learn to know what my needs are, and I would honor those needs. Emotional availability, expressing love, and honest communication topped that list. When I honored my needs, I'd honor my power. When I honored my power, I wouldn't relinquish my power to anyone else.

Third, I would always speak my truth—even if it was terrifying. I would never again stay in a relationship where love was withheld for fear of not finding someone who'd love me. I would never again cheat on a boyfriend because I didn't have the guts to say I wanted out. Truth-telling, always: that'd be my vow.

Fourth, if I do not know my truth, I would not search and look for it outside of myself. I would not turn to bottles of wine or emotionally unavailable men or fleeting experiences for answers. I would get very still and very quiet with myself until a hum of resonance emerged. And then I would act on that hum.

As I learned to do this, I learned to belong to myself. I learned how to honor my power and truth. And it was only then, when I belonged to myself, that years later, I was prepared for a conversation that took me by surprise with Farhad. After many weeks and months of business talk and friendship, and when we were (finally) on our first date and first glass of wine, he said, "I don't know how I feel about love." He spewed off statistics about divorce and talked about his friend's failed marriage. He shared that his last relationship was deeply troubling for him, and then he proceeded to intellectualize what love meant. I didn't buy it.

I could feel love permeating from his heart, and I could feel love permeating from mine. I could feel that love intertwining, and I could feel the possibility of what that might mean for us. I could sense that "love" came loaded for him with painful memories, profound expectations, and promises that could easily be broken. It wasn't that much different from that pivotal night with Jordan. Except *I* was different. I didn't know if Farhad was scared. I didn't know if he was falling for me like I was falling for him. This time I didn't care. My heart had already been shattered into a million pieces by Jordan, and because I had picked them up and put them back together one by one, I had the courage and guts to do what I did next: be my full unabashed wholehearted truth-telling self.

And so I launched into the most impassioned and heartfelt case about love. It was as if love were on trial for death, and I was its attorney. I held back in no way, telling him how love is something we must never withhold, and if there is anything we must do in this one lifetime, it is to love and be loved with all we've got. And when I had finished, and when I had taken a deep breath, and when I had swirled and sipped my glass of wine, which was appropriately named "Lil Lové," I watched as his face softened, his cheeks blushed, and the corners of his mouth turned upward. It's then that he looked at me in a way that I hadn't yet seen him look at me before. I cannot describe it in any other way except to say that in that moment I knew he had chosen me. And the reason he had chosen me was because I had chosen myself.

You can choose yourself too.

You can choose yourself every time you choose *not* to repress and hide and numb your true feelings. You can choose yourself every time you choose *not* to act like everything's okay and working when it's really not working and okay. You can choose yourself every time you oppose the guidelines of others when those guides do not make your heart pitter-patter with joy and delight and this-feels-truer-than-true-to-me. You can choose yourself every time that you choose to remember:

I belong to myself.
I am worthy of love.
I *am* love.

The WONDERVENTION

WAYS I'LL LOVE MYSELF:

- ☐ Journal
- ☐ Write A Poem
- ☐ Meditate
- ☐ Turn off my phone
- ☐ Take A Trip
- ☐ Feel my Feelings
- ☐ Say "I love you" to myself
- ☐ Smile
- ☐ Read A Book
- ☐ ____________

You Are Love

"THEY REJECTED ME . . . AGAIN." MEET DEFEAT.

"Another rejection," an artist texted me. "I'm feeling defeated."

"I totally get that feeling," I replied. "And, the trials and tribulations create a better story."

Think about it: if you were to read the biography of someone's life, and they experienced a perfect childhood with perfect parents, had perfect looks and were loved by all, and then their work went on to become an overnight success, would their story be very interesting?

I think not.

Interesting is Paulo Coelho being rejected over two hundred times before he went on to publish *The Alchemist*. It sold 65 million copies, was translated into eighty languages, and set the Guinness World Record for the most translated book by any living author. Imagine if he had given up at rejection 1 or 5 or 10 or 99 or 150 or 199? Sixty-five million people wouldn't have been touched by his work.

Interesting is a fourteen-year-old activist named Malala who overcame an attempted assassination by the Taliban when she was advocating every girl's right to an education. Rather than slow her down, it only sped up her vision of creating a world where every girl can complete twelve years of free, safe, and quality education—a mission that won her the Nobel Peace Prize.

The process of getting this book in your hands was interesting, too. After ten years of self-discovery and daily blogging, six years of message testing and refinement, thousands of clients and interviews, and multiple book proposals, I poured my heart into creating an eighteen-page document that represented the essence of the idea. From there, I reached out to a number of literary agents, one of whom said I was nowhere near ready to be a published author and I ought to go on an "egoless journey" before ever thinking about the book again.

Ouch.

As I took in his words, my hands began to tremble as a tidal wave of doubt rushed through me. The Worry voices in my head were having a hay day.

"He's right. You're not ready."

"You're not good enough to be an author, anyway."

"I told you not to put yourself out there."

As the worry storm tornadoed in my mind, I considered replying immediately in all capital letters: "WHO THE HELL DO YOU THINK YOU ARE, YOU ASSHOLE." The bottle of red wine in the kitchen looked real tempting, and I considered drinking the entire thing myself. Hiding under my covers was feeling like a viable option, too. As the critics continued to whisper, "You suck, you suck, you suck," it felt as if a crew of monsters had come into my living room, thrown me up against a wall, and put their hand on my throat in a choke hold. I could feel my throat closing and my vision blurring.

Just as I was about to succumb to the trappings of toxic worry, I paused and followed my breath. Inhale for four seconds, hold for four seconds, exhale for four seconds—just as I had learned in my mindfulness and breathing classes. When I did this, I was able to calm down, and observe my discomfort at a distance. Then, I named my shame to tame it.

"I see you," I said out loud—catching Worry off guard. "I see you, fear. I see you, anger. I see you, sadness. I see you, anxiety. I see you, doubt. I see you, shame. I get that you may feel hurt and scared right now. I get that you might suddenly think that our biggest dream is being swirled down the toilet. It's okay." As I spoke to my emotions directly, they released their grip. I shifted out of panic mode and came back to my center. I thought, "Okay. Worry tornado. I'm okay. Wonder, are you there? What's my next right move?"

It's then that I remembered the wisdom of my friend Jade Tailor, an actress on the hit Syfy network show *The Magicians*. Before she got her big break, she almost gave up. Over the course of eight years, she faced *thousands* of rejections, and no acting class had prepared her for the soul-crushing spirals of doubt that followed every time she got the call saying, *We've decided to go with someone else*. When I asked her how she managed to persevere, and what inspired her to keep going, she told me that she had to stop looking at it like rejection. Her job was preparing for the audition, showing up for it, learning from it, and improving her skills; it wasn't to win the role. She said, "They have a very specific idea of what they're looking for in the acting world, and you might not fit that. It's not personal; it's just not the right fit."

Her words *It's not personal; it's just not the right fit* comforted me with the rejection email I had just received. It didn't mean I wasn't ready. It didn't mean something was wrong with me. It didn't mean I am not good enough or unworthy. It didn't mean I should conceal and hide who I am to fit other people's description of who I ought to be. Hell no. It just meant that it's not the right fit. And my job was to keep showing up. To keep putting myself out there. To keep doing the work. To keep speaking my most raw and honest truth. And to expand and step even more powerfully into who I am and what I want.

I rooted myself in knowing my value, and I replied to the agent's scathing email as such. I let him know that "I heard his point of view, and it was clear that we're not the right fit." I thanked him for being so direct, and smiled knowing that his response saved me energy and time in exploring the relationship further. I hit Send, and I never heard from him again.

And then came the dozen outgoing emails that came next. Conversations that—because it wasn't personal—rooted me in reaching out from a place of looking for the right fit, rather than looking to "get picked." On the 333rd day of the year with thirty-three days left—a combination that felt like a "clue" that I was on the right path—I was introduced to an agent through a fellow author.

"AMBER RAE," she said on the phone, with a roar. "I've been SO EXCITED to talk with you. I was on the subway when I read your proposal, and I literally yelled out loud, HOLY SHIT THIS GIRL CAN WRITE."

I knew instantly she was the one, and the rest is history.

The theme here is resilience and trust. It's only by moving with the fear, doubt, and shame that emerges in the process of hearing "no"—and learning how to tune into the guidance of our inner truth instead—that we find the right "yes." This doesn't mean it won't be difficult or uncomfortable. Difficult and uncomfortable means that you're doing the important work and growing.

Take it from Liz Gilbert. When asked if her writing journey was easy, Liz said that she never asked her work to be "easy," she just wanted it to be interesting. "Because all the really interesting things in life are difficult," she said. "Love, wisdom, growth, compassion, learning, travel, loyalty, courage, endurance, transformation. . . . But 'interesting' doesn't mean 'tormenting.' When things get difficult, it doesn't mean that you have to suffer and moan and pull out your hair and rend your clothes. It just means things have gotten . . . well . . . verrrrry interesting."

Let "interesting" take you through every emotion you've been afraid to feel. Let "interesting" be the biography of your one wild and courageous life. Let "interesting" be a reminder that when shit is hitting the fan, it's yet another "interesting" moment that one day you'll look back on and laugh about. Like a friend once told me when she was going through hell, "As painful as this is—I get to experience it."

I get to experience it. I remind myself of those five words when I'm in the arena, getting my ass kicked. When I'm swimming in sorrow, and I can barely catch my breath. When I'm in the heat of an argument, and I want to run out the front door. When I'm feeling lost and confused and defeated and alone and afraid, and I'd rather not feel it at all.

I get to experience it. You get to experience it. We get to experience it. All of it. What a privilege. So let yourself experience defeat. And then get back up and go become better than anyone would ever allow you to be.

NAME 3 TIMES YOU PERSEVERED IN THE FACE OF REJECTION & DEFEAT:

1.

2.

3.

"WHO THE HELL AM I TO DO THIS? (I'M A FRAUD.)" MEET IMPOSTER SYNDROME.

On the next page is an actual entry from my journal *before* I fully committed to writing this book. Thank goodness for that pep talk at the end, or this book may not have made it into your hands. For many years, when it came to the projects that meant the world to me, the ones that I knew I must pursue, the ones that made my insides dance and my heart beat a bit faster, a huge terrifying question hung over me: "Who the hell are you to do this?"

I was too humiliated and afraid to let anyone in on this conversation inside my head. I thought they might think that I'm crazy, or they'd reinforce that *Yes! I am a fraud.* So I kept it to myself. I let it ruminate through my being, warp into my mind, and become my truth. My Modus Operandi. My Way of Being in the World (capitalized for dramatic effect).

Who the hell am I to write a book?! I don't have my masters in psychology. I don't have the credentials to offer "advice." I'm only 31 years old. If I do this, they might find out about me and call me a fraud. That would hurt. I probably shouldn't do this, right? I can keep helping others bring their ideas to the world instead. But Noooo! I can't keep hiding. I can't keep playing small. Yes, it's easier. Yes, it's safer. But my soul is literally DYING. I've been studying this for FOREVER. I AM NOT A FRAUD!!!! It is time to WRITE THE DAMN BOOK!!! Okay, okay. I'm writing the book. I'm giving it my all. Deep breath. It's GO TIME.

xo Arae

Thankfully, this distorted view of reality came into question the day I heard Oprah speak at the United Nations. Oprah said that after thirty-five thousand interviews, she observed that whether you're Beyoncé or someone who murdered their children, every interview ends with the same question: "Was that okay?," which really means, "Am I okay?"

And that's what we all want to know: that we're okay, and what we're doing is okay. That we're not a fake. That what we have to say has value for the world. That who we are is useful and worthy of love and connection. And for many of us, we fear that we're not.

Take it from Maya Angelou—the novelist nominated for the Pulitzer Prize and the winner of *five* Grammys. She said, "I have written eleven books but each time I think 'Uh-oh, they're going to find out now.' I've run a game on everybody." Seth Godin, after eleven bestselling books, said he *still* feels like a fraud in his book *The Icarus Deception*. Dr. Chan, the chief of the World Health Organization, said, "There are an awful lot of people out there who think I'm an expert. How do these people believe all this about me? I'm so much aware of all the things I don't know." The same goes for Sheryl Sandberg. In her book *Lean In,* she says, "Every time I was called on in class, I was sure that I was about to embarrass myself. Every time I took a test, I was sure that it had gone badly. And every time I didn't embarrass myself—or even excelled—I believed that I had fooled everyone yet again."

There's a name for this fear of being "found out." In 1978, two American psychologists—Pauline Clance and Suzanne Imes—created a name for the voice in our head that lives in fear of being exposed as a fraud: the imposter syndrome. They described it as a feeling of "phoniness in people who believe that they are not intelligent, capable or creative despite evidence of high achievement."

Maybe you can relate?

Journal into Wonder

What has Imposter Syndrome prevented you from pursuing? What evidence do you have to support that you're a "fraud"? What proof do you have that you're not?

My imposter syndrome was at an all-time high when a year after I started making art, my work was being featured in a gallery show alongside my two favorite street artists: Shepard Fairey and Banksy. The event coincided with my thirtieth birthday, and it was to be my first ever gallery exhibition. Naturally, I had only one question dancing around in my mind: "How the fuck did I get here?," which was followed closely by, "I don't deserve to be here."

It was a week before the big reveal, when I still had one final piece to create. My emotions were raging. I felt paralyzed by my fury of self-doubt. I seriously questioned backing out of the whole thing. I nearly wrote an email, telling the one hundred friends I'd invited that the show was off. It's then that I remembered the concept of "Inviting Mara to Tea," which I had learned from Tara Brach, a clinical psychologist and the author of *Radical Acceptance*. It's an approach for actively recognizing and learning to work with what we often consider "negative" emotions.

The story goes like this: The night before Buddha's enlightenment, he fought a battle with the demon god Mara, who tried to attack him. Mara failed but was only temporarily discouraged. He continued to try to wreak havoc and create harm with unexpected appearances. Buddha's attendant, Ananda, was always on the lookout to announce when the "Evil One" had returned. Instead of ignoring Mara or driving him away, the Buddha would calmly acknowledge his presence, saying, "I see you, Mara." And then he would invite him in for tea as an honored guest. Mara would stay for a while and then go, and Buddha would remain free and undisturbed.

This story reminded me not to push away and try to ignore my uncomfortable feelings—a strategy I had employed for most of my life—and to instead make friends with the demons in my mind. As an experiment, I grabbed a large printed photo that I had in the studio, and hand painted the stream of doubts in my mind on the paper.

I wrote, "Am I good enough? Will anyone like it? Am I out of my league? Why am I so afraid? What if I fuck up? What if they judge me? Who is 'they'? Can I pull this off? Am I ready? Is art selfish? Will my talent ever match my taste? I'm so terrified."

An interesting thing happened when I did this. The process of acknowledging my fear and doubt, and inviting them to move with me, enabled me to release the tidal wave of emotion inside, and turn my fears into poetry. The vulnerable words invigorated my creative process, and became the central theme of the art that hung in the gallery: four mixed media pieces showcasing the internal journey from worry to wonder. The final piece, which read, "I chose to see the world through a lens of Wonder, and everything began to BLOOM," contributed to how I uncovered the name to this book.

Funny how that works, right?

This story captures how we can respond to imposter syndrome when it flares up: we see it, we smile at it, and we invite it in for tea. We don't run from it, flee it, avoid it, or try to numb it. We befriend ourselves—all of us—and learn to practice understanding and compassion. We say, "I see you," and we keep moving—with the fears and beyond them. We create a new narrative: one that's rooted in our truth and power. It's the only way the gifts inside will see the light of day.

Journal into Wonder

What are the stream of doubts in your mind saying? Give your imposter a voice, and let it be heard. Exhaust every worry and fear. Use it as fuel for what you create next.

In the words of one of my favorite poets, Rumi:

This being human is a guest house.
Every morning a new arrival.

A joy, a depression, a meanness,
Some momentary awareness comes
as an unexpected visitor.

Welcome and entertain them all!

Even if they are a crowd of sorrows,
who violently sweep your house
empty of its furniture,
still, treat each guest honorably.
He may be clearing you out
for some new delight.

The dark thought, the shame, the malice,
meet them at the door laughing,
and invite them in.

Be grateful for whoever comes,
because each has been sent
as a guide from beyond.

The WONDERVENTION

THE IMPOSTER INSIDE MY MIND IS SAYING...

"I see you."

"I CAN'T DO THAT! THEY'LL JUDGE ME." MEET HIDING.

A friend of mine—an extraordinary memoirist of some renown—called me one day freaking out about her book. More than one hundred pages in, she had suddenly become frozen with fear. Her book was deeply personal, dark, and rich with vivid details of her twisted childhood. She was concerned about how the world would receive her, how her family would respond, and whether or not her reckless father—an alcoholic who abandoned her as a child—would come back to haunt her. Let's call her Gina.

"What if they disown me?" Gina asked.

Her inquiry is like many I receive. While each person shares in rich detail the extent and depth of their worries and fears—and how and why they cannot use their voice to speak their unshakable truth—the central question is always the same: *What will they think of me?*, which really means, *What if they abandon me?*

This is a question I have wrestled with tirelessly in my own life. Like Gina, it was when I was in the middle of writing this book—interestingly enough, about a hundred pages in—that I started to become awash with panic. My mind was racing with all the ways my writing could be condemned.

Moving beyond this noise required me to first remember Cheryl Strayed's advice that "There is the book you must write, and there is the book you must publish." They're rarely the same thing. Until we give ourselves the time and space to write what needs to be written, and express the oh-my-god-I-cannot-believe-I-am-putting-these-words-to-paper kind of truths, we won't be able to access the medicine of our own stories, and thus we may never know where to take the work. It's only after we've let our artist express itself fully that we can move into editor, packaging, and marketing mode. But before then, if we find ourselves feeling "stuck"—like Gina did and like I did, too—our paralysis may be a signal that we're hiding from ourselves and the kind of stories we ache to tell.

So go there. Enter the parts of your story that have felt too edgy to explore, and do so as vividly as you can possibly imagine. Maybe you will publish it, maybe it will serve only as a symbol of your own expansion. It's then and only then—when you've allowed yourself to divulge what needs to be told—will you know what to do with it.

Journal into Wonder

At the top of your page, write, "The thing I've been terrified to put words to is . . ." Let. It. Out.

Once you've had your whoa-I-really-needed-to-express-that catharsis, and once you're feeling clear on where to take the work, and once you're about to share it, you may find yourself worried about the fear of criticism. Gina certainly did. And I did, too. That's why I wrote a pep talk for all of us.

It goes like this:

Yes, they might judge you. Yes, their words may cut deep, and dampen your spirit. You may fall to your knees, while tears stream down your face. You may even find yourself wallowing on the couch for a few days, with a pint of ice cream, as you question everything about yourself, and what you're capable of. You may shut down, and feel as if the world is spinning around you.

At this point, you may wish that you had never made your voice visible. That you had never expressed that which you know to be true. You may then decide to quit, and to never return to your call to truth-tell. Maybe you'll take up and try out new hobbies and adventures. Or maybe you'll find quieter and less risky ways to use your voice. And maybe that will move you and stretch you and enthrall you to the same degree that your work once did. *Wonderful!*

Or maybe it won't. Maybe you won't find that same depth of connection. Maybe you won't feel that same extent of living out and walking your message that you once did. Maybe you won't feel as if you are watching yourself shift and evolve and grow right before your eyes in all the ways you know you are capable of shifting and evolving and growing. And if that's the case, your only choice then will be to return to the work that you know in your heart you're here to express.

When you learn to move beyond the voice of "What will they think of me?" and instead learn to listen to the voice of "What do I think of me?," you'll learn to rise above judgment and criticism, seeing it not as a reflection of *you* and your self-worth, but rather of *their* worldview. Because let's get one thing clear: **You cannot control how people perceive or respond to you.** A focus on *them* only takes you away from what *you're* here to do. There are over 7 billion people on this planet. Your job is not to please and receive approval from all of them. You will drive yourself crazy in that pursuit. Your mission is to express what only you can, and let that expression see the light of day.

It may stay as just that: an expression that came through you and out into the world. Or maybe it will come through you and find its way into the heart of someone else. Maybe it will move someone to such a degree that it spills through them with equal parts despair and delight. It might be the exact thing they needed to hear in that moment to see themselves more clearly. It might be the signal of hope, of letting go, of knowing that everything is going to be okay. It might be the spark, the catalyst, and the ignition for great change. It might turn them inside out and reveal to them a path they hadn't yet seen. It may reveal themselves to *them*. And you may reveal yourself to *you* in the process.

We don't know yet. But the only way to know, and the only way to find out, is to put all of you into the work, and then to set that work free. So show us your flaws. Dazzle us with how you moved through the darkness. Color us with all the shades of your life.

Yes, they might judge you. But who they're really judging is *themselves*.

the WONDERVENTION

IF CRITICISM AND JUDGMENT DIDN'T MATTER, WHAT WOULD YOU DO? SAY? FOCUS ON?

BE ALL OF YOU; NOT LESS

"OH GOD. LOOK AT THEM." MEET JUDGMENT.

I arrived at my hotel in Mexico, where I was traveling to lead a retreat. I headed to the rooftop to watch the sun set before the group arrived the next day. As I sat there joyfully, sipping mescal, taking in the sights and sounds, and reviewing my notes, I noticed a woman across the room. Among the bustling ambiance, laughter and cheers, she sat cross-legged in meditation for a good forty-five minutes.

"That's an interesting place to meditate," I thought to myself. And then she began to rise. She put her hands into a prayer at her heart, and she bowed. She bowed to herself. She bowed to the sun. And then she began to dance like no one was watching. Dance like she was in a moment of ecstasy. Dance like there weren't forty-some people in the place. Dance like it would be the last time she might ever be able to dance.

"What a show off," I thought to myself, while rolling my eyes. But still, I couldn't take my eyes off her. The whole place couldn't take their eyes off her, either. "She must really need the attention," I said to the stranger sitting next to me. "Should we tip her?" he said, laughing.

As discomfort surged through me—discomfort that she might be embarrassing herself, discomfort that I could never express myself that way, discomfort that she was so damn free and self-expressed—I was reminded of something my friend Wanda once said to me:

You cannot judge someone and love yourself at the same time.

Here I was, judging this dancing woman I knew nothing about. Judging this woman who had the courage to freely express her sensuality. Judging this woman who didn't seem to give a damn whether or not you watched or laughed or enjoyed or hated her performance. It wasn't even a performance; it was pure pleasure in motion.

That's when it hit me: I wasn't judging her. I was judging *me*.

Judgment is a mirror. A reflection. It shows you what you're denying and repressing inside of yourself. It illuminates where you're self-righteous. It's a map, pointing you to the place that you're afraid to accept within. As Carl Jung said, "Everything that irritates us about others can lead us to an understanding of ourselves." What we judge in others wants to be loved and embraced within us. It's an abandoned part of us calling out, "Hey! Pay attention to me! Notice me! Love me!" But so often we get caught directing our attention outwardly *at them,* and then we miss out on the wisdom that judgment is trying to deliver *to us.*

The dancing woman was so clearly shining a light of awareness on the areas of myself that wanted extra care. Like the part of me that was constantly concerned with how people perceived me. I feared that if I were to freely express myself in public—like this dancing woman—surely I'd be rejected and laughed at. And to do it in a sensual way? That might call the attention of men. That might bring on trouble or harm. Then it'd be "my fault." And if I got "too much" attention or shined "too bright," I would of course upset and hurt people, and I wouldn't be able to handle it.

Those were the worry myths the dancing woman brought to the surface for me to see myself more clearly. Those were the stories for me to lean into, and revisit. Just by being her. Just by expressing herself. *What a gift.*

I remembered the approach Wanda had taught me: when you notice yourself judging someone, tune into your heart, look at the person you're pointing a finger at, and say to yourself, "You are an aspect of myself. We are not separate. Thank you for the gift of awareness." I tried it on, and it worked. It helped me move out of the realm of judgment and back into the space of love and acceptance. For her and for me.

What about you? Can you think of someone in your life you're always pointing a finger of judgment and blame at? That you're always getting annoyed at and whispering criticisms about under your breath? Who was the most recent dancing woman in your life?

That person is your teacher. Your mirror. Your gift. That person is a signal for you to go within and wonder:

What am I judging in them?

What does that say about *me*?

Remember: They are an aspect of *you*. You are not separate. You are one and the same.

The WONDERVENTION

I'M FEELING ________ WITH
(emotion)

________ BECAUSE ________
(name) (situation)

________________________.

I WANT THEM TO ________
Her/HIM/
(ACTION)

________________________.

IF THEY DID, THAT WOULD HAVE
SHE/ HE/

ME FEEL ________________.
(emotion)

I CAN CREATE THAT FEELING

FOR MYSELF BY ________
(ACTION)

________________________.

WHAT THEY ARE REFLECTING IN

ME IS ________________.
(INSIGHT)

"They" are a reflection of *you*.

"ARE THEY A THREAT?" MEET JEALOUSY.

I suspect that, in theory, we all know that jealousy can destroy our most important relationships. But then come the times of actually coming face-to-face with this fact. It wasn't so long ago when I was writing in our Brooklyn loft, having a grand ole time, when I picked up Farhad's iPad to change the song. The precise moment I picked up the iPad corresponded with the precise moment a Facebook message notification popped up on the screen:

We had good times together, didn't we? ;)—Signed by Farhad's ex

From what I knew about their relationship, it had ended with a lot of heartbreak and pain. So seeing this message, I was immediately taken aback. I was so taken aback, in fact, that my heart started pounding out of my chest. And then came the next message five seconds later:

Yeah, we did. ;)—Signed by Farhad

YEAH WE DID?!!?!?! I thought. *WHAT THE HELL KIND OF GOOD TIMES ARE THEY REFERRING TO?!?!?! WHAT IS WITH ALL THE WINKING?!??! WHY IS HE RESPONDING TO HER SO GODDAMN QUICKLY?!?!?*

As I stood there watching their entire conversation play out, it felt as if someone had stabbed me in the gut, and dragged me across the floor. Before I could control myself, I was on his ex's Facebook page, obsessively checking what she was doing with her life to prove to my ego that I'm better, obsessively stalking her every picture, and then obsessively berating myself when I found pictures of her hard abs and narrow waist and tight little body, which had me feel like a soft pile of dough. Jealousy and rage pulsated through my veins as my nostrils began to flare and my body prepared for what felt like battle. I played out all of the conversations in my head and what I would say had I had the chance to jump through the screen and stand before his monster of an ex. What I didn't realize at the time is how much of a monster this situation had made *in me*.

Instead of breathing fire at her (an image that certainly flashed through my mind), I texted Farhad.

WHY THE HELL ARE YOU MESSAGING YOUR EX?!?!?!? I wrote—in my clearly cool, calm, and collected manner. *AND WHY ARE YOU RESPONDING SO QUICKLY???? YOU DON'T EVEN RESPOND TO ME THAT QUICKLY!!! BTW—DON'T YOU THINK FOR A SECOND THAT I'M BEING NOSY!!! I WAS ON YOUR IPAD CHANGING THE SONG*

WHEN THESE MESSAGES STARTING POPPING UP!!! I AM ANGRYYYYYY!!!!!

Farhad immediately called me.

"Babe," he said. "I understand why you're upset, and you have nothing to worry about. I love *you*. Yes, I responded to my ex quickly. But this isn't about you. It's about how hearing from her feels healing *for me*."

This isn't about you. This isn't about you. This isn't about you. Those four words played over and over in my mind like a boxing bell, punching me even harder in the gut than the good times he and the ex once had together. As a surge of jealousy shot from my gut up into my throat, I considered fighting back with rage. Instead, I took a deep breath, centered myself, and assessed the situation.

Yes, the conversation had absolutely nothing to do with me, and I was making it about me. Yes, I was making it about me because I was questioning whether his love for her trumped his love for me, and whether he thought her bod was hotter than my bod. Yes, his having good times with her in the past didn't mean that our good times in the present meant less. Yes, my fit of jealousy was leading us nowhere, and yes, if I were to respond with defensiveness and distrust, I would surely shut a door that I could instead open. I realized I had only one choice: to swing the door open.

"You're right," I said, in an actual cool, calm, and collected manner this time. "I'm totally making this about me. It has nothing to do with me. I'm so glad it's creating a space of healing for you. I love you, and I'd love to talk more about this later."

And as much as I actually *didn't* want to talk about this later, and as much as I would have preferred to push my reaction away as if it never happened (because I was actually quite mortified that it did), I remembered therapist Esther Perel saying that "the majority of people don't have a conversation about jealousy, because the feeling itself is taboo." And that's unfortunate, because jealousy is "a universal human emotion, one of many that is part of the multilayered experience of love." Unlike envy, which says "I want what you have," jealousy is provoked by "I have something that I think you want, and I'm threatened because you seem to be coming after it." And in that feeling of threat—which, when *listened to,* is actually a call to get closer—is a doorway to strengthen our relationships.

Keeping this in mind, when Farhad came home that evening, and when I had a hot minute to cool down and peel back the layers of my very irrational, insecure, and jealous response, I brought it up, and we had a big laugh at the whole situation. And in our giggles and in my flushed-with-embarrassment cheeks, I saw a chance to lean in to greater intimacy and connection. With a loving gaze and curious heart, I asked about Farhad's past, the relationship that shattered his heart, and how he pieced it back together. The next several hours were spent with him sharing the ins and outs of their relationship, why he felt drawn to her, what made him feel hurt, and the insecurities that were brought to the surface when they broke up. By the end of the evening, an interesting thing happened: we were holding each other closely and tightly. We were gazing deeply into each other's eyes. And an explosion of love and connection was erupting in our chests. This was all because I didn't allow my jealousy and my insecurity and my fire-breathing rage to take power over me. Instead, I transformed them into a deeper kind of intimacy and connection that we had only scratched the surface of before.

And isn't that the point of tension in love? Pausing when you're acting like a monster yourself—a monster that's keeping you from going deeper and deeper and deeper—and retracing your steps?

Yes, it is. And yes, it's always available to us when we choose to swing the door open rather than swing it shut.

Swing it open, always. As wide as you can.

The WONDERVENTION

THE LAST TIME I FELT JEALOUS WAS...

HOW I RESPONDED IS...

THE WAY I WANT TO RESPOND NEXT TIME IS...

LET JEALOUSY BRING YOU CLOSER TOGETHER

"WHAT THE ACTUAL FUCK." MEET ANGER.

After years of people pleasing and performing, when I was learning to say no, I had an interaction with a stranger that pushed me to my edge. Let's call him Rich.

Over the course of a week, Rich sent me five emails asking me to write an article for his company that was just about to launch. After I wrote a piece about a friend's company, and it went viral on *Fast Company,* he had seen me referenced on Tim Ferriss's blog for how to "hack Kickstarter." So thus began the era of receiving a dozen or so emails per week from guys like Rich. Emails that were seldom well researched. Emails that were rarely thoughtful. Emails that seemed to consider only one thing: how great they were. When I began getting more emails than I could keep up with, I made a rule: If they don't take their time to do their research, I won't take my time to reply. It worked like a charm for filtering through the noise.

But then came Rich. When I didn't reply to Rich's request that I write about him because "it was the next big thing" and "I would surely regret it," he emailed me again. And again. And again. He kept emailing me to tell me what I was missing out on, and how I'd better jump on board. When I didn't reply to his emails, he began tweeting at me. "Did you get my email?" he asked. "You have no idea what you're missing out on!"

"No, Rich. I don't know what I'm missing out on because you didn't make a strong case for why I should care. I'm not interested, thanks!" is what I thought but didn't send. And then, days later, I ran into him at an event. "You're Amber Rae!" he yelled when he saw me. "You're the girl who knows nothing about email etiquette! You only care about yourself, don't you?" Then he started laughing. Then the group he was with started laughing. I was so shocked and taken aback by what felt like public shaming that I froze. I couldn't form a coherent sentence. Words literally were not coming out of my mouth. I began shaking. I turned the other way, and ran.

When I got home, I called a friend. As I paced back and forth around my apartment, yelling, "HOW DARE HE!" and "WHAT AN ASSHOLE!," my friend said, "Wow, it sounds like you're really angry."

"I'm not angrrrryyyyyyyy," I said, while throwing my journal across the room. I really didn't want to be angry at Rich. I wasn't the kind of person who got angry. I'm a *nice* person. I keep it together. I make sure everyone is happy and doing okay. Nice people don't throw tantrums. Nice people smile and nod and pretend everything is oh-so-great. But everything wasn't oh-so-great. I was pissed the fuck off.

I had become so accustomed to repressing my anger. Ignoring it. Hiding it. Denying it. Running away from it. Self-medicating it. Doing everything but *listening* to it.

Maybe you can relate?

But now I was in the early stages of learning how to turn toward my emotions—learning how to be with them rather than flee from them—and all kinds of uncomfortable shit was coming up to the surface.

"Anger is our friend," as I learned from Julia Cameron in *The Artist's Way*. "Not a nice friend. Not a gentle friend. But a very, very loyal friend."

Anger erupts through us, and it speaks—loudly. Anger is a signal. A call to get curious. Anger slaps us across the face, and says, "Listen. Something isn't right here. Something needs your attention. And it needs your attention RIGHT NOW." Anger shows us when a boundary has been crossed. It lets us know when what we've been doing is no longer working. It tells us when we've been betrayed and when we are betraying ourselves. Anger is an invitation to act. Not to *act out* our feelings, but rather to *act upon* the message beneath them.

"I had the idea for Instagram first," a dozen or so entrepreneurs have told me—pissed off and seething. "It's so simple. It's just an app with a photo stream. I could have done it, and I could have done it *better*." That was anger speaking through them, saying, "Stop delaying. Stop putting off your ideas. Apps don't become billion-dollar companies overnight. Go put in the work."

"Oh god—another friend got engaged," a friend said to me, rolling her eyes. "It's so annoying and I'm so fed up." That was anger speaking through her saying, "You want love. Admit it. Put yourself out there. You deserve it."

"Those jerks stole my idea," an artist told me after a major brand took her signature piece of work, repurposed it, and started selling it on T-shirts. "What the actual fuck." That was anger speaking *loudly,* saying, "Boundary crossed. Absolutely not okay. Respect your work, and do something about it."

So she did. She hired a lawyer. She told her community and they stormed the brand's Instagram feed. They sent the company letters. She spoke clearly and loudly saying—This is not okay. If you want to use my art, here are the terms. They took down her work, put out an apology, and hired her. That engagement ended up leading to a big break in her career. All because she listened to anger, and she did something about it. She didn't act out, she acted *upon*. And there's a difference.

Acting out is when you take your rage out on people you love. It's when it becomes your friend or your boss or your lover or your roommate or your company's fault when something isn't working. Acting out is when you punch a wall or throw a fit because you've been betraying yourself, and you're sick and tired of it. Acting out is what happens when you've been stuffing feelings inside of yourself for years, and some offhanded comment sends you spinning into a fury of rage.

But acting upon is different. Acting upon is wise. Acting upon ensures that we change what needs to be changed to ensure that our needs and wants and best interests are met. Acting upon is how we value ourselves and prioritize our well-being. Acting upon starts with, "What message does my anger have for me?" and ends with, "And what am I going to do about it?"

When I got off the phone with my friend after the run-in with Rich, I picked up the journal I'd thrown across the room. I opened it, and began to write.

"What message does my anger have for me?" I jotted down.

My anger is telling me that his behavior is not okay with me. I feel disrespected and humiliated. I feel like I did something wrong, even though I know that I didn't do anything wrong.

My anger is telling me that I'm very, very, VERY triggered by him saying that I only care about myself just as I'm finally learning how to honor myself. He touched on one of my deepest fears of being seen as selfish.

My anger is telling me that I want to be able to speak my truth and use my voice—clearly and calmly—in situations when I feel voiceless and hesitant and scared.

"And what am I going to do about it?" I wondered next.

I'm going to use my voice. I'm going to act upon my anger by reaching out to him, telling him what happened for me, and how our interaction upset me. I'm going to practice the techniques I learned from studying nonviolent communication to write him a note. And I'm going to do it now.

I opened my laptop, and wrote:

Hey Rich,

When I saw you at the event, and you said that I only care about myself, I froze. Here's why: My tendency is to overcommit myself and people please, and I'm trying to break that pattern. I have a hard time saying no, and it's something I'm working on. So when I received five emails from you in one week, and in those emails you only spoke about your company, I felt disconnected from your work. The more you reached out to me, the more disconnected I felt. Because I value choice and because I created a sense of pressure every time you wrote to me, I was not inclined to support you or even respond. I have a rule for myself: If they don't do their research on me, I'm not going to reply. So, if you have an ask in the future, my ask is that you do some background research and show me how we're a fit.

Best of luck with your launch.

Cheers,
Amber

I never heard back from Rich. But it didn't matter—I didn't need to know that he heard me. I had heard myself. I had *listened to* my anger, and acted upon it, rather than acting on it.

So the next time you're pissed off and raging, remember this: Anger is your very loyal friend. A friend who'll do whatever it takes to get your attention. A friend who will continue waving a red flag until you look within, and ask yourself:

1. What is your anger trying to tell you?
2. And what are you going to do about it?

Act upon; not out.

The WONDERVENTION

1. I ACTED OUT MY ANGER WHEN I...

2. MY ANGER WAS TELLING ME...

3. TO ACT UPON MY ANGER, I WILL...

ACT UPON YOUR ANGER; NOT OUT

"NO PAIN, NO GAIN." MEET SUFFERING.

I once had tea with a musician who said to me, "I don't date women I could fall in love with because then I'd have nothing to write about. I go after women who I know will hurt me." The drama, the tension, the struggle, and the pain were the source of his greatest music.

Or so he chose to believe.

The story of "suffering to create" is one a dear friend of mine also once believed in fiercely. Let's call her Celine. The process of bringing her ideas into the world was always painful and borderline masochistic. As a designer, she believed that if she wasn't nearly killing herself to cross the finish line of a project, she wasn't being productive enough. If she wasn't working with demanding clients, she wasn't challenging herself enough. If she wasn't losing sleep and clocking in ninety-plus hours per week, she wasn't pushing past her discomfort.

When I asked Celine where she learned this story of achievement, she told me a mentor once said to her: "If you're not suffering, you'll never produce anything great."

Now, to some degree, I understand what her mentor was trying to say. Maybe he meant "Embrace the discomfort," or "Don't be afraid to go beyond your edge," or "Suffering is a natural part of creating anything." But to suggest that greatness only emerges through suffering is not only untrue, it's also disturbing.

But Celine believed it.

She bought into the story of her pain more than the story of her enjoyment. So when clients and projects came along that actually sparked her curiosity and made her feel excited, she pushed them away. She felt guilty at the prospect of feeling enthusiastic about her work. She didn't trust in joy as a path to learning, growing, and becoming the kind of designer she wanted to be. She believed with all of her being that the only path to success came through struggle. There was no other way.

Journal into Wonder

What did you learn about suffering growing up? What role does it play in your work and life?

Celine's story is not rare. Far too many people have been taught to place suffering at the center of their work and life. Maybe you, too, were taught to believe in your struggle above all else. Maybe pain and pain alone is the only way you've known how to grow. When I was in high school, a family friend always said to me, "No pain, no gain." Even though I respected him, I had a hard time taking his words to heart. Pain never seemed to bring him closer to the kind of life he actually wanted to be living. I knew my father—a gifted songwriter—battled addiction and a number of ailments trying to bring his music to the world. He too believed in drama and pain as a reliable source for writing music. But look where that took him: to the grave.

I wanted to believe in a different story. One rooted in joy and love. One that allows delight to sit at the center. One that believes significant work emerges through significant play. One that is enamored by the mysteries of existence and the wonder and awe of this chance at life. This doesn't mean ignoring suffering and pain and struggle. Those are unavoidable parts of the human experience. What it means is that we don't have to seek it out.

Awe and wonder can be hard to see when you're in the midst of nearly killing yourself to reach an end goal. I heard a story from author and entrepreneur Jeff Goins about how he bootstrapped his company to a million dollars, and then found himself living in the stressful reality of running a seven-figure company. With the support of a coach, he built out a meticulous two-year strategy, and thought: *Okay, my life is going to suck for a couple of years while I grow this, and then I'll get out of my business and do what I really want.*

But as he worked the plan, his anxiety grew. His love for the work decreased. He stopped working on the craft he loved most. He spent less time with his family. He started losing money, which triggered his deeper fear about going bankrupt. In the midst of his struggle, a call with Seth Godin changed everything.

When Seth asked why he started the company, he said, "I wanted freedom." Then Seth said something Jeff will never forget. He said, "Don't build a business because you want freedom. Build a business because you want to run a business."

He didn't want to run a business, he realized. His kids were six months and four years old, and he knew he'd miss out on their lives trying to grow something he didn't intend to do for the rest of his life. So he decided that bigger wasn't better for him; smaller was. He adjusted his plan and scaled back. He began spending more time with his kids. He started writing more. Within six months, he experienced more freedom and felt more joy. By revisiting what was most important to him, he learned to trust in his joy and spend time on the activities that actually gave him the sense of freedom he was looking for. You too can choose freedom and joy over suffering and pain.

Listen, I know sometimes life can be challenging and scary and anxiety inducing and heartbreaking. I've been through my seasons of shame and blame and misery and feeling like life-is-most-definitely-falling-apart. But what I've found is that it is nearly impossible for me to do the kind of work I'm capable of when I am miserable, in a frenzy, staying up late, making things harder than they need to be, and proudly wearing that struggle like a badge of honor.

Am I getting more done? Absolutely not. Am I writing? Hell no. Am I moving closer to who I ache to be and what I want to create? Nah. Am I holding on to my story of suffering as an excuse for why I'm not creating the things I want to be creating? You better believe it.

More often than not, I notice that **we're afraid to lose our suffering because we're afraid to lose our excuses**. It's easier to hold on to pain as a reason for why we're concealing our gifts, playing small, and not going after the kind of life we want to be living.

But trust me on this: you are so much bigger than your suffering and pain. No matter what happened yesterday, or what might happen tomorrow, you have right now. In this exact moment, you are all right. You are breathing. Your future awaits you. Face this moment with strength. Face your excuses with courage. Be kind. Trust in joy. Love over pain, always.

The WONDERVENTION

WHAT WOULD IT LOOK LIKE TO PUT LOVE & JOY AT THE CENTER OF WHAT YOU CREATE? WHAT MIGHT CHANGE?

LET *love* LEAD THE WAY

"I'M TERRIFIED OF GOING THERE." MEET AVOIDANCE.

Four and a half years into my relationship with Farhad, the fire of desire we once had began to fade. A part of me feared that we were meant to love each other up until this point, and then let go. We had held a container for each other to heal inner wounds and step into our power. He was an embodiment of the masculine love I craved, and a reliable and stable figure that loved me unconditionally. He was always there. There for me when I didn't know how to be there for myself. There for me when I was afraid to face my demons. There for me when I was spewing with insecurity and self-doubt, and hiding under the covers. He looked at me, and within me, and saw a greatness and light that I would sometimes question within myself. He nudged me gently in the direction of my dreams. He supported me in all the ways you'd want someone to support you.

Under the surface of this idyllic relationship existed a truth that I was too afraid to look at: our sexual connection. When it came to desire in our relationship, something felt missing for me. I wanted him to throw me up against a wall and . . . you get the picture. I wanted him to own his sexual power, to enchant me and mesmerize me and tantalize me. Instead, we filled our days with long stretches of cuddling and tender embracing and baby voices. We joked we could win awards for the length of time we spent in each other's arms. But the primal sexual part? It was absent. I felt so ashamed by this very fact that I refused to acknowledge it. Because if I did, it might mean something was wrong. Wrong with me. Wrong with us. *Wrong.* The prospect of being honest, and the chaos that might erupt into our relationship, felt frightening. Terrifying. Unbearable. Plus, I had important work to do. So rather than move into the discomfort of a difficult conversation, a conversation I feared would have him feel like he wasn't worthy or enough, and a reaction that I feared I wouldn't be able to handle, I threw myself deeper and deeper into my work. I acted like everything was okay. I had sex simply to check the box of having sex so that he wouldn't think anything was wrong.

And then I met a man I'll call Sebastian. The spark of connection I immediately felt with him awoke in me a surge of sexual desire I didn't know I was capable of accessing. I felt seen, felt, and captivated in a way I hadn't experienced with Farhad in a while. His level of presence and the way he peered into my eyes sent arousal pulsating through my veins. At one point, the turn-on reached such a peak that I considered sleeping with him. It was then that I saw Farhad's face. It was then that I remembered the man who loved me tenderly and deeply. It was then that I chose to maintain the integrity of our relationship by sleeping on it, rather than sleeping *with him*.

My interaction with Sebastian remained a figment of my imagination. A possibility uncharted. A fantasy unexplored. A darkness I feared entering. As I reflected on the feelings that emerged, and the connection that I allowed myself to feel into, a profound sense of guilt came over me. Our society's chains on female sexuality, and the shame of pursuing pleasure, weighed on me heavily.

I worried:

Am I a bad partner?
Does this mean I'm unfaithful?
Do these fantasies mean something is wrong with me? With us?
Is wanting to explore the depths of my pleasure bad?
Is our relationship ruined?

A part of me felt liberated by the sense of desire and sexual connection I felt, whereas another part of me felt wrong and bad for allowing myself to feel it. I battled the permission I wanted to give myself to connect more deeply with my sexual energy, and what those desires might mean to the man I love dearly.

Sebastian was a mirror into my own dormant desires and turn-ons. A way for me to see what I'd been afraid to explore, to admit, to feel, to access. It felt edgy and dangerous, just as it feels edgy and dangerous writing this to you now. And in that edginess, and in that danger, is a truth that I know more truly than any other: the path forward is to always speak and live out my wild and honest truth.

And so I chose to step into this by having a wild and honest conversation with Farhad. I was terrified. There was no detail I wanted to leave unsaid, no feeling I wanted to leave unexplored. Transparency was a core value in our relationship, and I wanted to honor that. But how would he take it? How would he receive my truth? How would he respond to my eruption of desire? He was going through a pivotal time in his career, and I feared my sharing might throw him off. I worried our relationship might implode and destruct and send us spinning in opposite directions. I felt concerned that my words might reinforce his myth that he is not good enough or worthy of big love. True love. You-are-my-person kind of love. When I sat in front of him, and looked deeply into his soft, kind, and caring eyes—the kind of eyes that *knew* something was up because of how well he knew me—a rush of hesitation moved through me. It's then that I remembered my commitment to myself: **I didn't promise myself a comfortable life, I promised myself a true one.**

So I told him everything. I shared what felt missing between us and what I felt ignited with Sebastian. I told him what Sebastian said, how he made me feel, and how, for a fleeting moment, I wanted him. I showed him our texts, and shared the play-by-play of our rendezvous. As I spoke honestly and frankly and directly and passionately, I watched as his expression of devotion turned into despair and his despair into pain. My-heart-just-got-ripped-out-of-my-chest kind of pain. My-ripped-out-heart-just-got-handed-to-me kind of agony. I watched him, for the first time, question if our love would last. I watched him, for the first time, want to run and hide and leave and eject from the conversation. I watched him shut down, and disconnect from his emotions. I watched him create a wall between him and me. As we stood on two sides of that wall, I searched to find a door to open to get to the other side. The side where I could be near him and close to him and embracing him. I looked for a window to step through and a rope to climb. Every time I found a door, he shut it. Every time I found a window, he locked it. When I ran for the rope, he pulled it up. He was shutting me out, and doing so quickly. He was shutting me out because he had convinced himself that I had made up my mind. That he and I had run our course, and I was ready to move on without him.

In some ways, he was right. We had reached an end. We had reached a death in our relationship. But it wasn't the ending or the death he had fabricated in his mind. It was the ending of avoiding hard conversations. It was the death of acting like everything was okay when it wasn't okay because we loved each other so much and feared that what was not working might break us. And what I realized, most of all, is that if I wanted to have this love last, if I wanted to keep my vow to choose him every day no matter what came our way, I would have to learn to stop looking outside of the relationship for solutions to what I was wrestling with on the inside.

While Sebastian seemed alluring and exciting and shiny on the surface—and may have led to a fleeting experience of erotic eruption—what he illuminated even more clearly were the deeper issues at play in my relationship with Farhad. I recognized a crossroads: I could hide from the challenges I had become so good at skirting, or I could face them, bring them to the surface, and approach them head-on. I again remembered my commitment to a true life, rather than a comfortable one, and so I wholeheartedly chose truth.

Journal into Wonder

Where in your life have you been pretending that everything is okay when it's not? What's the payoff of pretending?

It became apparent in this exploration process that Farhad filled a void of secure, stable, and fatherly love in my life. He comforted my inner child—the part of me that feared abandonment like one fears death—by having me feel unconditionally loved and cared for. He deeply accepted and embraced all parts of me, including the parts I struggled to accept, embrace, and love. Through the way that he loved me—the way I never felt a father love me—he showed me ways to love myself.

Being in this kind of entanglement had served us up to a certain point. It was safe and beautiful and had me feel sheltered and cocooned. But, we also recognized that this kind of involvement was unlikely to serve us in the long term. It was unlikely to lead to the depth of sexual connection we longed for, and the kind of power and strength we knew we were capable of as a couple.

As we sought counsel from specialists, we learned from sex therapist Esther Perel that even the prospect of betrayal can create the painful end of a chapter in a relationship, but it doesn't necessarily mean that the whole thing is done. "Your first relationship is over," she said. "Would you like to create a second one together?" We did, so we made new agreements—mainly, that we would have the hard conversations. We would expose what we'd rather cover up. We'd walk hand in hand into the ache and the uncertainty and the pain. And we'd count on each other to illuminate everything that is unresolved within us.

As we did this—as we surrendered to aspects of our relationship falling apart so they could come back together—we learned to harness and embrace the energy of conflict, and come through it transformed. Our old relationship may have had a death, but we emerged reborn. Alive. Invigorated. *Closer.* I recognized that I am the source of whatever connection I experience outside of me, and I get to choose where I channel that flow. I vowed to choose Farhad, and he vowed to choose me, too.

That's what's possible when we meet avoidance and allow it to transform us.

It can be hard and heartbreaking—I get it. When what we're thinking, feeling, or experiencing is too uncomfortable, the only way we may know how to deal with it is to avoid it. If it's too painful, we may try to escape it or fix it, thinking it will go away or lessen in severity. It can involve *doing* something—like working harder so you don't have to face uncomfortable feelings, not putting yourself out there so you don't have to face rejection, or having that extra drink to take the edge off. It can also involve *not doing* something—like avoiding a challenging conversation, creating distance between you and someone you feel in conflict with, or trying to convince yourself that what you want isn't all that important anyway.

The problem is that when we use avoidance to cope, we only strengthen our anxiety and we usually end up experiencing more of whatever we were trying to flee from in the first place. The path forward is to see our avoidance and anxiety as a signal to act. An opportunity to choose what's true over what's comfortable. A chance to step into courage while holding ourselves with compassion. It's our moment to write our bravest ending yet.

The WONDERVENTION

① I'M AVOIDING...

② BECAUSE...

③ WHAT I NEED IS...

④ MY NEXT MOVE IS...

AVOIDANCE IS A CALL TO BE COURAGEOUS

"THERE'S NO WAY I CAN HANDLE THIS." MEET OVERWHELMED.

An entrepreneur wrote me, asking, "I'm finally following my biggest dream. I left my corporate job, started my own company, and I'm making progress every day. But I'm constantly paralyzed by a fear that I'm running out of time (and I'll never have enough of it), I won't be able to make payroll, and everything is going to go to shit. At my worst, I begin questioning whether or not I made the right choice to do this and whether or not I can handle it. Do you have any tips on how to deal with the paralyzing anxiety?"

A traveling writer and Instagrammer wrote me around the same time, asking, "I'm finally getting paid to do the thing that I love (travel the world! write about it! take photos! create Instagram campaigns with brands!). But there's one problem: I'm so overwhelmed. Unforeseen challenges keep showing up, which sends me into panic mode. It's hijacking my creative process. It's making me a shitty writer. It's making it difficult to face each day. The self-doubt is so intense, and it's making this big dream that

I've worked so hard for feel way too stressful for me to enjoy. Have you faced this?"

Oh, yes. Big time.

I learned a whole new approach to facing the feeling of being overwhelmed through the Japanese martial art aikido. It's a form of self-defense that is often translated as "the way of unifying (with) life energy." When I took a class with a sixth-degree aikido black belt, one thing became very clear very quickly: If I try to run away from conflict and chaos, I will be defeated. If I panic, I will get hurt. If I start doubting my power, I will be overpowered. The path is to face chaos in a calm, constructive, and centered manner. To sense the energy that is coming at me, and come into union with it.

As I learned from my teacher, the process of becoming a black belt comes with a final test called the *randori,* which in Japanese means "taking chaos." Dripping in sweat and exhausted from previous attacks, the candidate stands at one end of the mat while multiple attackers, all black belts, rush forward in quick succession without knowing how they will attack or in what order. By staying centered, taking steps forward, tuning in to the energy patterns of the group, and facing challengers one at a time, the candidate can defeat their opponents. However, getting caught up in any one opponent for too long or losing touch with one's center will cause the candidate to be defeated.

These same principles apply when we are becoming a master at our craft, and walking along the path that we've worked so hard for. Whether we're facing a big deadline or dealing with unexpected forces that come our way or are paralyzed by mental drama, the ultimate test is how we navigate the chaos. Because there will always be periods of it.

Panicking, shutting down, running away, or jumping into stories about what the chaos means invites defeat. Breathing, holding a relaxed and flexible posture, sensing into your center, and approaching each challenge one at a time invites victory.

When we're aiming for our best work, when we're wanting new and novel ideas to emerge, when we're facing hard deadlines that are unchangeable, the task is to learn to aikido them—to unify with the energy of challenge, and stay calm through the chaos.

Because showing up to create anything is an ebb and a flow. A dance. Periods of immense flow are followed by periods of deep questioning. And experimenting. And refining. And editing. And doubting. And clarifying. And internal excavating. All of which is eventually followed again by clarity and flow. What matters is that we continue to show up—whether or not we're afraid, whether or not we think we're capable, whether or not we know what's coming next, and whether or not we have a voice telling us "this is too hard and too intense and oh my god, did I make the right decision?" When we choose to pursue that which we desire, there are so many unknowns, and those uncertainties can be terrifying and overwhelming. As I heard angel investor and entrepreneur Naval Ravikant say to Tim Ferriss on his podcast *The Tim Ferriss Show,* "Desire is a contract you make with yourself to be unhappy until you get what you want."

Whoa. Let's repeat that one more time: **Desire is a contract you make with yourself to be unhappy until you get what you want.**

And what we often want is to get to the end. To reach the goal. To cross the finish line. To make strides forward. To know how the money is coming in, to know that we have enough time, and to know how to deal with our unforeseen challenges. But the process of creation asks something of us first: to get comfortable not knowing what will happen and when. Because creation is messy. It's raw. It's foggy. It's vulnerable. It's illuminating. It brings all kinds of shit to the surface. And it's precisely when we tend to want to run the other way, and it's precisely when we must stay. For it's there that we discover treasure.

This is why we must ask ourselves whenever we choose to do something that we feel is worthwhile: *Am I willing to get uncomfortable in the pursuit of what is mightily important to me?* Because when we are, we will persevere to uncover lessons and gifts. But only if we continue to show up, and take the next step forward and the next step forward and the next one after that. Again and again and again.

It's when we learn to relax our shoulders and return to our place of stillness within, approaching each challenge individually and face on, that I believe this with all of my being: **Desire becomes a contract we make with ourselves to *respect the process* as we move toward what we want.** But only when we learn to aikido the shit that emerges along the way.

Aikido that shit. Let it show you your remarkable resilience. It's a test. An initiation. And this I know: you're stronger than you think.

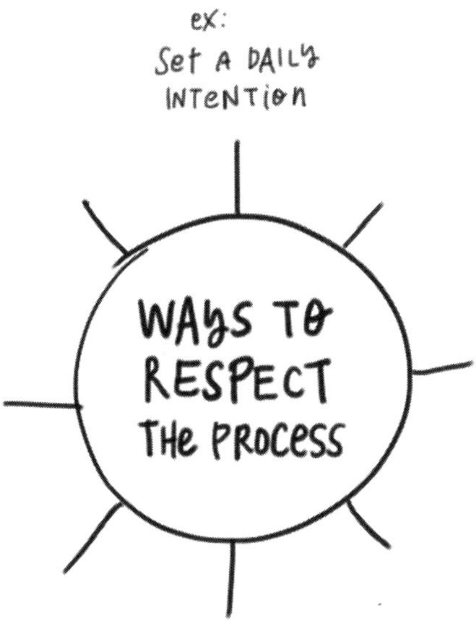
ex:
Set A DAILY INTENTION
WAYS TO RESPECT THE PROCESS

"MY MIND IS RACING." MEET ANXIETY.

You know those moments when a storm is brewing inside your mind?

You're trying to choose Wonder, but toxic Worry is spinning out of control. You don't know how to slow down your thoughts or come back to your center. The regret, disappointment, and I-should-have-done-that-differently rumble through your being as truth. Fears about what could go wrong send your mind racing. As the thoughts combine, intertwine, and weave a web of worry, your breath shortens. Your heart beats faster. All you hear is noise. Deafening and paralyzing noise.

It's a sensation I've encountered frequently in my life.

Maybe I'm working on a project that is near and dear to my heart, and I'm suddenly certain that I'm going to disappoint everyone, make a fool out of myself, and the entire project is going to fall apart. (*Am I really worthy of what I desire?* I think.)

Or I'm scrolling through Instagram, where everyone's life seems perfectly put together, and I'm quite convinced that I'm behind and doing life wrong. (*What the hell am I doing with my life?* I worry.)

Or maybe I'm losing sleep because the world feels in shambles and the unpredictability of what happens next is making me sick. (*Is our world going to fall apart?* I fear.)

Or maybe my life feels so out of control that I'm on the floor, shaking, and in a full-on panic attack. (*Why is this happening to me?* I scream.)

If you can relate, you're not alone. We live in the "Age of Anxiety," as the *New York Times* reported, where we swipe our iPhones mindlessly, looking for that missing dose of happiness. We pack into meditation spaces, hoping to quiet our mind. We read books like this one, hoping we'll crack the code for the void we feel inside. With so much pressure to live our greatest lives and unlock our fullest potential—and do it all by the time we're thirty—it's no wonder so many of us feel anxious.

Whenever I speak about this topic, the first question I'm asked is, "How do I make my anxiety go away?"

It's a question I'm all too familiar with, and it's one I've asked myself mightily over the years. It's also the question that doesn't make our anxiety go away, it only makes it grow in size. Just as "don't panic" or "stop worrying" are two of the least helpful things we can say to someone who's in the middle of a panic attack, having that same intention with ourselves is only going to intensify our pain.

The very nature of aiming to make our anxiety "go away" sends us seeking solutions outside of us for the discomfort we feel inside. We have a glass of wine or pop a pill to take the edge off. We dive more deeply into our work and fill our lives with more commitments. We up our ambitions and goals, as if by reaching them, our angst will decline. We do everything but FEEL our anxiety, which is exactly what is being asked of us.

Anxiety is not your foe, it's your friend. Your very nervous, yet very devoted friend. The friend who taps you on the shoulder in the middle of the night and says, "Hey, you. Something isn't right here. Something feels out of alignment. Sorry to freak you out, but it's the only way I know how to get your attention." When you sink beneath your spinning thoughts, shortness of breath, and racing heart, you'll discover your voice of wonder. You'll hear your inner truth and intuition saying, "Hey, you. Pay attention. It's time to realign."

Because on the other side of our anxiety is our alignment with the path best suited for us.

Realignment doesn't come from running from our anxiety or trying to change it. It comes through embracing what's true, and listening to where our anxiety is pointing us.

So when anxious thoughts come up, here's what I suggest:

1. Use a mantra to calm racing thoughts.

When my mind is racing, and I'm on the verge of spinning into panic, the first thing I'll do to calm my nerves is repeat "Wonder over Worry" until I calm down. Our anxiety is self-inflicted and a result of our own preconceived limitations, and this mantra brings me back to my center. Research also shows that mantras reduce activity in the part of our brain responsible for self-judgment. And when we're feeling anxious, less self-criticism is precisely what we need.

2. Name it to tame it.

Then, I'll pull out a sheet of paper and write all my anxieties down. The act of writing reduces our racing thoughts because when they're bouncing around inside our minds, they feel chaotic, messy, and intangible. By acknowledging what we're feeling in the moment, we put a face to our discomfort. We create a distance between ourselves and our emotions, so we can see what we're working with. As Dr. Daniel Siegel said, "Name it to tame it." Neuroscience research shows that when we do this, we reduce the charge of our anxiety immediately. For example, when I think about my biggest dream, my chest tightens, my breath shortens, and a bunch of thoughts fly through my mind like "What if I mess up?" and "Am I good enough to do this?"

3. Prevent anxiety through morning journaling.

As a preventive measure, every morning I wake up and start the day with what Julia Cameron dubbed "morning pages." It's a practice I've had for nearly a decade, and it is, by far, the most impactful twenty minutes of my entire day. "Morning pages" are three pages of stream-of-consciousness writing. It's a safe space to express all of your worries, doubts, and fears, and move them from noise in your mind to feelings on a sheet of paper. It creates distance between you and your anxiety, and gives everything you're feeling a name and a face. I also find it helps me let go and trust, and thus answers to my biggest questions tend to pop up naturally on their own.

Journal into Wonder

Set a timer for ten minutes and try on "morning pages." At the top of the page, write, "Right now, I'm feeling . . ." Let it flow.

4. Schedule time to listen to your anxieties.

So much of our angst comes from resisting our anxiety. Allowing ourselves to feel what's there to feel allows us to move beyond the noise. Intentionally set aside time to listen to your anxieties to see what's beneath them by asking yourself questions like: What is out of alignment? Where am I feeling off track? What conversations am I avoiding? What feelings am I pushing away? What is asking for my attention? What is my anxiety wanting me to know?

5. Use anxiety as fuel.

Channel what you feel into what you create next. Heartbroken about a relationship? Write a poem about it. Outraged at the state of the world? Start a dinner series to talk about it and create an action plan. Overwhelmed with everything on your plate? Paint your feelings. There is power in your emotions, so learn to use them as fuel. Do this by asking yourself, "How can I channel this energy into creating something useful?"

Creating alignment in your life is a process, and it doesn't happen overnight. As you uncover what does and does not work well for you, you will take steps forward and back. It's a process of experimentation, trial and error, listening, channeling, and adjusting. Be kind with yourself as you make shifts, fall short, and figure out what works best *for you*.

And remember: anxiety is a messenger wanting to bring you back to your center. Turn toward it, rather than away. Work with it. Use it as fuel for what you create next and you'll get out of its way.

THE WONDERVENTION

IF MY ANXIETY IS A SIGNAL THAT SOMETHING IS OUT OF ALIGNMENT, WHAT IT'S TRYING TO TELL ME IS...

ANXIETY IS YOUR FRIEND, NOT YOUR FOE

"THAT DIDN'T GO HOW I EXPECTED." MEET LOSS.

The relationship fell apart.
The idea didn't take off.
The proposal got denied.
You got onstage and forgot your lines.
The business failed.
You lost a chunk of money.

When things don't go as we would have expected or liked, we may be inclined to brush it off, let it go, and move on quickly. We may be inclined to secure a "win" as quickly as possible to get a temporary boost of feel-good confidence. But when we're always moving from the next thing to the next thing, we can miss out on the important growth that comes through mourning what we've lost. While we may think we're making progress and creating strides, these scars—when unaddressed—can block the channel of creativity, stifle our relationships, and lead to unresolved grief.

I experienced this firsthand when I worked with a writer to co-create a book project that was near and dear to both of our hearts.

When the idea to collaborate dawned on us, she flew to New York and we set up camp in my loft. Over the course of a weekend, we filled nearly every square inch of the floor with four-by-six notecards, which led us to create an outline for the book and finish the first rough draft. I had every reason to be excited, and yet I suddenly felt paralyzed by doubt. As my voice, my value, and my ability to follow through all came into question, I froze. I stopped showing up fully to the project, and she ran with her part of the idea. I'm glad she did, because it went on to be a big hit and bestseller.

But then came the turn of events that I wasn't expecting. The more I told myself that it wasn't a big deal, and I was happy she got to make it and it got to be made, I noticed something interesting: I wasn't able to write. And the more I brushed it off and acted like I was totally unaffected by it, the more affected I became. And the more I tried to secure the next win and the next win and the next one, the more empty I felt inside.

When we're dealing with loss of any kind, we may think in theory that we can move on quickly, when in reality, what we're triggering are old wounds. A relationship ending may evoke the same sense of abandonment we felt when Dad left for a trip (or forever). A creative project failing may invite the same pain we felt when our artistic tendencies were shunned. Running out of money may invite the same stress we felt when we saw our parents fight about not having enough. If we try to move on before we've grieved what's there to be felt, we'll keep repeating the same patterns again and again. Loss says, "Hey, I'm hurt. I'm feeling a little achy right now. Please be extra kind and patient with me right now. Please hold me and love me and pay attention to me." And since we live in a society that tends to want to fast-track that grief, and get back to happy as soon as possible, it's important that we learn to pause and be with it. Because when we do—when we create the space to acknowledge our pain and ache and regret—that's when we can move beyond and rise above the grief. It was only when I felt my sadness and disappointment all the way through that I was able to open a fresh page and begin my own book.

Journal into Wonder

What loss have you not allowed yourself to grieve? Why have you been avoiding it?

So when loss happens (because it always will), here's what I want you to remember:

Grief, pain, and heartbreak have their own timeline, and take time to unravel.

When we try to move forward and onward as quickly as possible as a means to get back to feeling good, it will only cause *more* pain and suffering. The aim is not to numb or silence what we feel, but instead to learn to *listen*.

It's okay not to feel okay. It's okay to feel sad. It's okay to be overcome by grief. Rather than try to overcome your feelings, learn to be with them. To stay. To allow. To feel your feelings and your grief and your pain all the way through, and right to their origin. When you can illuminate where your story begins, you can have compassion for the part of you that's triggering past pain. Connect with the hurting you inside, and say, "I'm here. I'm with you. It's okay. Let's feel this."

People we love may think that they are loving us by telling us to "move on," "get over it," or "feel better" faster than we're ready. (I know because I've been that person.) Any attempt to rush you through your process so you can "heal" is a projection of their inability to deal with their own discomfort and pain. It's a reflection of their own unresolved emotions, unmet sadness, and abandoned pain. Now is the time to surround yourself with people who hold you, love you, meet you where you are, and show you that in your pain is the path forward. Now is the time to hold yourself that way, too.

Above all, remember this: Feel your loss. All the way through. And when you do, it's then and only then that the next two questions are this: What did I gain from this loss? And where is it pointing me next?

Because loss, when unresolved, is a block. But loss, when grieved? It's a powerful force of creative energy that wants to move, and it wants to move *through you*.

THE WONDERVENTION

1. THE LOSS I HAVEN'T GRIEVED YET IS...

2. THE REASON I'M AVOIDING IT IS...

3. TO GRIEVE & FEEL IT FULLY, I WILL...

"I'M RUNNING AWAY FROM MYSELF." MEET ADDICTION.

An addiction to Adderall almost killed me. But you would have never known that.

From the outside, it probably looked like my life was perfect in college. I was excelling academically. I was in a relationship that others envied. I was thin and considered attractive. I had an internship with Apple and my work had been featured on the front page of my university's magazine. I had high hopes for my future, and so did most everyone else.

So how did I find myself naked on the floor, shaking uncontrollably, as my Adderall-racing heart sent me into a seizure?

Why did I continue to hide behind my addiction well into my midtwenties, and at my lowest, steal pills from a kid and forge fake prescriptions?

Why is it that so many people face debilitating addictions like I did, and never seek help?

Where It All Began

Years after my father's accident, my mom remarried and on their wedding day, I decided to call this new man "Dad." At first, their relationship was a dream. But then it started to fall apart. To cope, I tried to control everything in my life.

My grades. My body. My relationships.

I would eat an entire pizza with my boyfriend and then use laxatives to eliminate. When laxatives didn't seem to do the trick, I stopped eating. By the time I arrived at college, I was living off of sugar-free Red Bull and iceberg lettuce. Oh, and liquor. Lots and lots of liquor.

Drinking wasn't my thing in high school, which I made up for when I got to university. I developed a ritual my freshman year: Study all day; drink all night. Binge eat at night; take a laxative. When I came home for the holidays, my mom gasped at how frail my figure had become. I assured her it was my newfound passion for working out.

My Hidden Secret

When the new year came, and the study/drink/starvation cycle had become exhausting, a friend handed me a pill just as the night was getting started. "What's this?" I asked. "Adderall," she replied. That pink pill changed everything for me. Once it kicked in, I was overcome with euphoria. All of my fears vanished instantly, and all at once. I could talk to anyone. I didn't care what anyone thought of me. My appetite was cut. I'd parade around the dance floor, feeling as if I were on top of the world.

A week later, I sat front and center with a psychiatrist, telling him about my "inability to focus" and the "symptoms" I knew he wanted to hear. Thirty minutes and three hundred dollars later, I had a 60-mg-per-day prescription to Adderall. If you're not familiar with the dosing, that's three times the amount that can kill a small cat. And just like that, Adderall became the secret drug that erased my insecurities, filled my hole of inner emptiness, and made me feel worthy and enough.

But for every momentary high came the sleepless nights, my always speeding heart, and an inability to tap into and feel my emotions. With every pill I popped, it marked a scar on my heart: "Hurt myself again." My better knowing and judgment and light were so clouded by a substance that I had convinced myself was making my life better. But it wasn't making my life better. It was making my life a living hell.

That hell came to a halt when I got caught forging prescriptions at a pharmacy. Rather than call the police, the pharmacist called my former doctor. He said he'd call the authorities, and for whatever reason, I never heard from him again.

But the fear of that phone call put me in a prison. The irony is I had put myself in a prison all along. Adderall was a crutch. A way for me to mask my insecurities rather than face them. I wasn't just addicted to Adderall, you see. I was addicted to the false sense of connection and love it made me feel in my life. That's the feeling I was actually looking for when I twisted the cap off the prescription bottle and swallowed a pill.

British journalist Johann Hari, in his widely popular TED Talk "Everything You Think You Know About Addiction Is Wrong," suggests that the opposite of addiction is not sobriety; it is connection. I couldn't agree more. It was only through cultivating a sense of true connection and acceptance for all of my shortcomings and flaws—and being able to share my struggles with those I felt safe with—that I was able to climb out of my hole of addiction and despair.

As I faced myself, I stopped needing to hide from myself. I stopped needing to hide from my life. As I honored my creativity and talents, I learned to see my inner angst as fuel. Fuel to create. Fuel to write. Fuel to express what was dying to be born through me.

Addictions As a Blocking Device

Some of us come to addictions because of the momentary flicker of ecstasy. The escape. The desire to touch peace and joy. The need to run away from our pain. For others, it's when we begin to sense our true potential and the glimmer of possibilities that await us.

The deal happens. The relationship is blooming. The career is skyrocketing. Your truth is being revealed in precisely the way you always imagined. And it's then that we may be swayed to seek addictions as a means of self-sabotage.

Knowing yourself means acknowledging what you abuse when you want to hide from your power. Honoring yourself means realizing that what you abuse is likely the thing you will most defend. "A drinking problem? Never. Not me!" I said for years, as I poured myself that third glass of wine rather than sitting down to write.

What is it that you reach for? What is that you defend? What is it that you're afraid to admit?

Is it alcohol to take the edge off? Is it sugar and junk food that makes your mind fuzzy? Is it staying busy, busy, busy, and adding more and more to the calendar because you're confusing your work with your self-worth? Is it a relationship you obsess about? Is it sex that you turn to when you want to avoid the real work? Is it the critical inner chatter? Is it scrolling mindlessly through Facebook?

None of these things is destructive on their own, of course. It's the misuse of them that stifles our potential. It's when we reach for blocks as a way of turning against ourselves, our truth, and our power. Rather than allowing ourselves to experience the freedom and joy that come along with trusting our intuition and our gifts, we numb ourselves. Staying small is easier to swallow than stepping into who we've always known we're capable of becoming.

As we create awareness around the ways we numb, we begin to move beyond our addictions. We notice when our actions are out of alignment with our true desires. We begin to trust in our gifts more than our dependencies. We learn to see our addiction for what it is: a strategy for running away from ourselves. We learn to turn toward ourselves, accept ourselves, be kind toward ourselves, and forgive ourselves. We learn to use our real emotions as fuel for our work rather than an uncomfortable part of ourselves we tend to deny. We learn to release our shame and speak up.

Journal into Wonder

Let's get real. What habit gets in the way of your creativity and power? How do you numb yourself? What is the payoff? What do you plan to do about it?

Speaking Up

I questioned mightily whether or not to include this essay in the book. I struggled looking in the mirror and speaking the words, "I was addicted to Adderall." I feared it might shift your perception of me. I asked Farhad dozens of times if he was sure this topic was a good fit for the book. I almost chose that third glass of wine over finishing it. I almost deleted the entire thing before finally inserting it in the manuscript at the last minute.

With every excuse for why not to share this story came a truth I couldn't ignore: **The silence around addiction is what keeps so many of us stuck.**

Whether it's you or someone close to you, many of our lives have been touched by addiction, and keeping these stories concealed suggests that there is a reason to be ashamed. When we feel ashamed, it makes it that much more difficult to speak up and face ourselves.

Seeing that I took myself to hell and back because of addiction, I am here to tell you: you have nothing to be ashamed of. We turn to addiction when we're afraid, and we don't know where else to turn. Staying silent will only strengthen your pain. Real courage comes when you first admit to yourself that you have a problem, and then when you have the strength to seek help.

Your addictions may not kill you. But staying silent about them could.

I've met many people who've struggled with addiction at some point in their lives, and what I can tell you is this: They are some of the most extraordinarily creative and sensitive and brilliant people I've ever known. Because they didn't know how to channel their gifts, they learned to dim their light instead.

You can stop dimming your light, and you can stop right now. Because beneath your addictive behaviors is a wellspring of creativity and talent and potential that is bursting at the seams. What you crave is seeking an outlet of expression.

It all begins with naming what's in your way, and then facing it.

Face yourself. It all starts with you. And it begins now.

The WONDERVENTION

LET'S GET REAL.

THE HABITS THAT BLOCK MY GIFTS ARE...

THE PAYOFF IS...

MOVING FORWARD, I WILL...

TRUST IN YOUR GIFTS

"I MUST NEVER MAKE MISTAKES." MEET PERFECTIONISM.

Perfectionism sucks the joy out of living and creating. It's self-sabotage at its finest.

At its core, perfectionism is fueled by the underlying belief that "I am not good enough (or thin enough, smart enough, rich enough, successful enough, or ________ enough)," and I need to try harder and harder to get *there.*

It's limiting and unattainable, wrapped up in a story that our acceptance and lovability are rooted in whether other people perceive us as perfect. With an eye on *them,* we aim to never reveal our flaws or make a mistake. Because then we would be unworthy.

I know the limitations of perfectionism all too well. My need to be perfect developed from well-intentioned teachers, family members, and strangers validating me for being "pretty" and "such a good student." This led me to believe that "pretty" and "high performing" meant *worthy of love*.

As a young teenager, I believed that if I "had it all together," I could create peace and stability amid the messiness of life. I turned to magazines and the media as a model to construct who I was or *wasn't* supposed to be, which only further disrupted my sense of self.

This led to an endless list of goals: 4.0 GPA, dean's list, restricted diet, be thin (always), be well liked by all, have a perfect relationship, get into the best college, make everyone happy, and always be positive. And then—as if that wasn't enough—I was to continue striving to do, be, and achieve more, handle it all with grace, and never stop to take a breath along the way. My relentless striving led me to make strides in my career left and right. Strides that I wore proudly like a badge of honor as evidence to others that I was enough.

The reality is that I lived in a cycle of self-judgment, where my every mistake was yet another marking of my unworthiness. It was as if, in every moment, I was keeping score of my value. Check, check, check—"not worthy or deserving of love"—I'd mark down every time I fell short of my unattainable and unreachable goals. This left me feeling so numb and *out of control* that I desperately tried to control everything else around me. I was terrified of being seen for who I really was—as a real individual with strengths *and* flaws. I was afraid that if I wasn't perfect, no one would ever love me.

Brené Brown says this addictive belief system is fueled by a primary thought: "If I look perfect, live perfectly, and do everything perfectly, I can avoid or minimize the painful feelings of shame, judgment, and blame." And the reason this cycle is so destructive is because "when we invariably do experience shame, judgment, and blame, we often believe it's because we weren't perfect enough so rather than questioning the faulty logic of perfectionism, we become even more entrenched in our quest to live, look, and do everything just right."

Sound familiar?

	PARALYZING PERFECTIONISM	HEALTHY STRIVING
MISTAKES =	I'M FLAWED	I'M GROWING
UNCERTAINTY =	I'M DOING IT WRONG	I'M FINDING MY WAY
ASKING FOR *help* =	I'M NOT ENOUGH	BETTER, TOGETHER
YOUR WORK =	NEVER GOOD ENOUGH	EVOLVING & IMPROVING
FLAWS =	UNLOVABLE	HUMAN

It was in my endless "hustle for self-worth"—as Brené calls it—that I had a conversation with a lover in my midtwenties that I'll never forget. We had only been dating for a few weeks, and we were in the I-want-to-spend-every-second-with-you stage of love. This particular afternoon was his first time coming over to my place, and rather than share the nervousness I felt around our blossoming relationship, I walked him through my every accomplishment in life, even pulling out my "achievement folder" for visuals. It was when I began placing magazine cutouts on my bed that he stopped me.

"I really want to know about your life," he said, placing his hand on my shoulder. "But you know you don't have to list off your accomplishments for me to love you, right? You don't have to be perfect for me. Your internal conflicts are just as interesting."

I remember that moment vividly—the way I was leaning up against the bed, the red folder I was holding in my hand, and the way he looked me in the eyes—because in that instant, he struck my deepest and darkest fear, and held a mirror up to it. It felt like he reached into the depths of my soul, yanked at my deepest insecurity, and revealed to me in his hands the guts he found. I was mortified. It had never before occurred to me that I believed I had to be perfect to be loved. His words struck such a chord, and illuminated such an undeniable truth, that I considered running away or ending the relationship right then and there. Instead, I froze. My years of acting and performing for love flashed in my mind like a movie. The relentless striving, the unnecessary suffering, and the grasping for approval at every turn all came crashing down as a man stood before me claiming that he wanted to love me *for me*. Not the image of who I thought I should be. *For me*.

I was stunned.

You don't have to be perfect for me.

I didn't have to be perfect for him, even though parts of me were terrified to believe that could even be true. I could show him all sides of me—the broken, hesitant, and messy parts—and he was willing to embrace and be with it all. My lovability did not depend on whether I succeeded or failed. It depended on the woman inside.

And the same goes for you.

Have bold visions and dreams for your life, please. Aim to be the best you that you can possibly be. And, have the courage and willingness to let them shatter you, open you in ways you didn't know you could open, and reveal to you the fragility of what it means to be human. And then amid the uncertainty, the angst, and the tenderness of it all, let it belong to you, let it nurture you, and let it fuel what you create next. Let your flaws not be a signal that something is wrong with you, but evidence of how human you are.

Your internal conflicts are just as interesting.

I have learned this over and over and over again. First came the resistance to loving my cracks. And then came the day when I decided to own my flaws so I could write the ending. I went to an art show with the new boyfriend who had reached into the depths of my soul and exposed my cracks. While there, I saw a piece of art that drew me in like a magnet. It was a piece of pottery, shattered and broken and glued back together with gold lacquer. As I traced my finger along its bumpy contours, sharp edges, and soft porcelain exterior, I found myself taken by the object's unique beauty. The process didn't hide the cracks, or the fact that the pottery shattered. It embraced those imperfections to create a one-of-a-kind piece of art that was even more unique.

That pottery, I learned, was inspired by the Japanese art *kintsugi*. It's a process that celebrates breakage and repair as part of the history of the object—a history to honor and revere, rather than disguise and hide. Kind of like our lives.

While the events of our lives may cause us to crack, shatter, and fall apart, when we tend to our fragile parts, and handle them with openness, love, and compassion, our lives become a unique piece of art that never would have before existed.

The goal, then, isn't to mask our flaws or return to a state of perfection. It's to own, honor, and come to a place of comfort and peace with our cracks. Because it's there we will find our place of enough.

Let me ask you this: How have you been defining "enough" up until now? Does enough mean a certain weight on the scale? An amount in your bank account? A specific number of Instagram followers? Does it mean going to the best parties and having the respect of a certain kind of crowd? Having people perceive you in a certain way? Accomplishing every single item on your bucket list?

Because here's what I learned the hard way: Those things don't make you enough. They sent me chasing after the next thing and the next thing and the next thing—with no end in sight. I got *there,* and then I thought, *This isn't what I thought this would feel like.* I expected to feel happy and whole and complete, but instead I felt empty. Lifeless. Exhausted. Turned off. Drained of my life force and livelihood. And ashamed. Ashamed because I put all that time and energy into getting *there* and now I felt . . . not much of anything.

When this feels difficult to swallow and admit, instead of questioning the definition of what's "perfect" and "good," I kept chasing. I kept running. I jumped back on the hamster wheel, and I kept looking to fill the void of enough through doing more, and trying to do it perfectly. And in doing so, what's blurred was my ability to see what is so clear to me now: **That I was already enough. That you are already enough. That enough is our birthright. That enough is who we are and who we've always been.**

Enough is always there, waiting for you to play with the possibility of it being true. To pause from the never-ending quest of reaching an unattainable ideal, and to instead wonder: *If I believed that I am truly enough, what would happen then? What would shift? What would I do? How would I express myself? Where would I go? If I were to embrace the wildness and messiness of it all, what might I become?*

You are enough. Let those three words be a bright light in your darkest hours.

You.

Are.

Enough.

The WONDERVENTION

MY OLD DEFINITION OF ENOUGH (WHICH HAS ME FEEL CRAPPY):	MY NEW DEFINITION OF ENOUGH (WHICH HAS ME FEEL <u>ALIVE</u>):

YOUR LIFE. YOUR DEFINITION.

the UNION

PART THREE

MEET WISDOM

Up to this point, we've made a great case for Wonder: the courageous, curious, and compassionate part of us that guides us through our worry myths to unlock who we truly are and what we have to offer the world. And it's when we do that—it's when we learn to turn toward our emotions, be kind to ourselves, and live a life that is more strongly led by Wonder than Worry—that we are introduced to another voice: **Wisdom**.

Wisdom is the part of us that sees value in Wonder's grand and glorious plans with Worry's more watchful and careful eye. Wisdom is adept at hearing what Worry has to say without spinning into panic, while simultaneously tuning in to where Wonder's curiosities are pointing. Wisdom knows it's not an *either/or*—or a game of right and wrong and good and bad—it's an *and*. It's a holding of both. It's a reverence for all of our contrasting and contradictory parts. Because while Worry without Wonder is paralyzing, toxic, and unproductive, Wonder without Worry is impulsive, overactive, and usually overcommitted. That's where Wisdom comes in. When Wisdom runs the show, Worry and Wonder respect each other, move as allies, and walk hand in hand in the direction of what is most aligned and true. It's called **The Union**.

The Union is when we welcome fear, sadness, grief, shame, joy, heartbreak, vulnerability, and unworthiness to all have a seat at the table of our heart. It's when we invite every part of us that we've denied, repressed, or abandoned to come forth and join us. Not so that we can "fix it" or "make it better" or "overcome it," but so that we can acknowledge it and embrace it lovingly for what it is: an aspect of who we are. When we do this, we tap in to a wellspring of creativity, connection, vitality, and flow. This is the place from which our greatest contributions, deepest connections, and most profound experiences emerge. This is the place from which we return home to who we are.

"I AM HOME." MEET WHOLENESS.

Many years after my father died, when I was in my late twenties, I found a letter he had written to me when I was an infant. I was with Momma, going through old treasures, when we uncovered my baby book. Inside the book were stories about the joy Momma experienced with me month after month, my never-ending quest to be naked, and of course my first word: "Da Da." It was clear Momma wasn't thrilled about that one, because next to "Da Da" she wrote *Boo! :(*

As we kneeled on the ground next to each other, laughing with wells of tears in our eyes, I turned the page to discover something I never expected to find: a letter from my father. When I held that letter in my hands, I felt a kind of joy and elation and heartache that I cannot describe in any other way except to say that in his cursive handwriting and on that parched paper, I felt as if I were transported to the moment in time when he wrote it, and I touched his soul.

I devoured his words like a hungry and ravenous animal that hadn't eaten in months. I analyzed his every sentence, and his every word choice, hoping that by taking it apart, I could piece him back together in my heart. Reading his advice to always "live out the truth of who I am, and not who others wanted me to be" sent shivers down my spine because it felt like he knew me without ever *knowing* me. His remark that "no matter what happens, he'll always love me" had me feel like in some small way, when he wrote me this letter, he knew what was so achingly true: that one day, I would read it without him.

After reading his words forward and backward and inside and out, I hugged it and embraced it and held it close to my heart as if I were hugging him for the first and last time. The letter was the only tangible artifact I had from his life. The only expression of who he was and who he aspired for me to be. I had spent so many years of my youth playing make believe in my head, imagining what he would have been like, what he would have taught me, how he would have interacted with my boyfriends, and what he would have said at my wedding. And now, in my hands, I held a piece of him. I held a piece of *me*.

When I held that letter close to my heart, I had a profound realization. It dawned on me that growing up without my father led me searching to fill the hole of him, without ever knowing there was a hole to fill. I tried stuffing accomplishments and wine and the love and approval of men into that hole because I thought that by doing so, the hole would go away. But it didn't go away; it only increased in size.

That hole, I learned quite painfully, would never be filled by anything or anyone outside of me. Not in my relationships with men, not in how I looked and appeared to others, not in empty prescription bottles, not in what I could or could not accomplish, and not in the letter I now held in my hands. As much as I wished there was a shortcut around this—a shortcut to feeling and experiencing his unconditional love—there wasn't. It was when I came to terms with the heartbreaking fact that I would never find my father and I would never fill his void that I began the journey home to myself.

The void of him is part of me, and the work was not to deny it, but to embrace it. The work was looking at the void, and saying: Thank you, void. Thank you for your confusion and your pain and your gaping hole in my heart. Thank you, gaping hole in my heart, for sending me on an all-consuming quest for love and approval outside of me. Thank you for being a part of me. Thank you for teaching me and growing me and thrusting me into the realization that my father is not out there, he is *in me*. That love is not out there, it is *in me*.

It was when I learned to stop seeing every interaction through the lens of *Do you love and approve of me?* and instead through the lens of *Do I love and approve of me?,* that I learned how to climb out of the hole that I was so accustomed to digging myself into. And when I climbed out of that hole, what I found is what I had always ached to feel but never knew I was looking for: **wholeness.**

Wholeness didn't come through denying any part of myself, or trying to shift or change or transform or heal my cracks. It came through taking all the parts of myself that I was rejecting, and saying: I see you. I see you, abandoned little girl. I see you, inner wild child. I see you, ashamed and unworthy and afraid and shaking. I see you, voiceless. I see you, unlovable. I see you. I love you. I accept you. You are part of me. You will always be part of me. You are welcome here. Thank you for being here. Thank you for teaching me. I will carry you home.

The Union of all of my parts is how I came home to myself. And it's how you too can find your way home.

YOUR JOURNEY BEGINS RIGHT HERE, RIGHT NOW

As we embrace the fullness of who we are, the expression follows naturally.

As we move with the mess, the mess becomes our message.

As we listen to the clues guiding us, the work that wants to be made comes through.

As we share our gifts, doors open where they previously did not exist.

As we walk deeper into the core of who we are, we realize that in every moment, in every conversation, in every dead end, and in every moment of wonderment is a clue. A guide. A signal. Something outside of us illuminating a truth within.

And as we pay attention to these truths, and piece them together, what we create is a beautiful quilt of our own making. A painting that only we could paint. A story that only we could write. A journey that only we could take. A home within ourselves that we are always welcome in. A home where we can rest and share our gifts.

Let's mark this moment with a commitment to living your wild truth. To welcoming all of who you are. To making the right next move. To seeing Worry, and choosing 1 percent more Wonder. To knowing you're worthy, regardless of what happens next. To being ready, because the life you're intending is already on its way.

LIVING MY WILD TRUTH: MY COMMITMENT

I, ______________________________, am devoted to living a life that is more strongly led by Wonder than Worry. I commit to living out the truth of who I am, even when—and especially when—it's terrifying.

While I have many curiosities that I'd like to uncover and pursue and express in this one lifetime, over the next thirty days, I intend on fully devoting myself to ________________________.

At the end of thirty days, I will feel alive, successful, and over the moon when I:

Knowing this, my most important next three moves are:

1.
2.
3.

I understand the power of honoring myself and knowing my needs (so I don't burn out), and I commit to practicing self-care through ______________________________________.
When the going gets tough or I'm drowning in worry, I'll reach out to ______________________________________ for support.

Let's do this. I'm all in.

____

Signature   Date

- the conclusion -

THE END IS THE BEGINNING. THE END IS THE BEGINNING, THE END IS THE BEGINNING. THE END IS THE BEGINNING THE END IS THE BEGINNING. THE END IS.

When I got to the last page of this book—a moment that I've spent most of my life imagining what it would feel like—my first thought was, "I don't know if this book is good enough."

And I just started laughing. Like fall-to-the-floor, tears-in-my-eyes kind of laughter. Laughter because I expected some grand moment of fireworks and revelation upon getting to that last page, and laughter because this was actually quite perfect in its imperfection.

We make things; we question them.

We put our whole hearts into something; we wonder if it's enough.

We let go of how it will be perceived; we focus on what feels true.

We learn to ask better questions; we expand into that inquiry.

We release our work into the world; we let go of our attachment to its outcome. (Or at least we try.)

We make more things, and the cycle continues, walking us deeper and deeper into our truth within.

This is the dance of expressing the fullness of who we are and what we have to give. It's terrifying and exhilarating and dark and light and messy and spacious. It's all of these things—all at once. As we hold space for these contradictions, we hold space for ourselves and our gifts.

When I stood up from my fit of laughter, I thought, "Oh, hey, Worry. Thanks for that nod of encouragement," which was followed closely by, "Wonder?! Are you there?! (Please don't leave me hanging.)"

As I looked around my villa in Bali, taking in its every color and detail as if to frame the moment in my mind forever, the most profound sense of gratitude and joy and rapture moved through me. And in that moment, the song that was playing changed, and the philosopher Alan Watts began to speak through my speakers. I got the sense that maybe we did get our moment of fireworks after all.

In the words of Watts:

If you awaken from this illusion
and you understand that black implies white
self implies other
life implies death
or shall I say death implies life,
you can feel yourself.

Not as a stranger in the world.
Not as something here on probation.
Not as something that has arrived here by fluke.
But you can begin to feel your own existence
as absolutely fundamental.

What you are basically,
deep, deep down,
far, far in, is simply,
the fabric and structure of existence itself.

Let's suppose that you were able every night,
to dream any dream you wanted to dream.
And that you could, for example, have the power
within one night to dream seventy-five years of time.

And you would naturally,
as you began on this adventure of dreams,
you would fulfill all your wishes.
You would have every kind of pleasure.

And after several nights
of seventy-five years of total pleasure each,
you would say, "Well, that was pretty great."

But now, let's have a surprise.
Let's have a dream which isn't under control.
Where something is going to happen to me,
that I don't know what it's going to be.
And you would dig that.

And come out of that and you'd say,
"Wow, that was a close shave, wasn't it?"

Then you would get more and more adventurous
and you would make further and further gambles
as to what you would dream.

*And finally you would dream—**where you are now.***

Right now there is an energy, a gift, a vitality just dying to be expressed through you. Because you are you, and there is only one of you, that expression is unique. Rare. Distinct to you. And waiting to be born.

The only question that remains then is this: Will you let it be expressed?

I hope you say *Yes*. I hope you CHOOSE WONDER.

A FULL AND GRATEFUL HEART

To my agent, Sarah Passick. I adore you for getting me and this message immediately, texting me into the wee hours of the night, and being your fine and fierce self every moment of every day. Thank you to Celeste Fine, Anna Petkovich, and the entire team at Sterling Lord Literistic. You all amaze me.

To my editors, Alicia Clancy and Hannah Braaten—it was such a joy and honor working alongside you. Your commitment and devotion astounds me. To Karen Masnica, DJ DeSmyter, Staci Burt, Sara Goodman, Anne Marie Tallberg, Anna Gorovoy, Olya Kirilyuk, and the entire Wednesday Books team—I love the magic we've made together.

To team Wonder—Kellee Tarum and Tony Bacigalupo—working with you brings me deep joy.

To KC Baker—you helped me uncover and birth this message. My gratitude is beyond words.

To Liz Gilbert, Elle Luna, Susie Herrick, and Andrew Horn—you were catalysts for me to prioritize this project with my whole heart.

To the many book muses whose guidance and support has meant the world—Laura Griffiths, Majo Molfino, Azzurro Mallin, Carmina Becerra, Quddus Philippe, Liz Presson, Ezzie Spencer, Colleen Waterson, Kate Jones, Gina Golia, Tobias Rose-Stockwell, Liz Flores, Michael Lipson, Amit Gupta, Dhru Purohit, Seth Godin, Sam Horn, Nathaniel Koloc, Adam "Smiley" Poswolsky, Baldwin Cunningham, Teri Kelly, Liz Brown, Misha Hyman, Wanda Badwal, Allie Mahler, Shannon Jamar Sangster, Christine Lai, Jason Anello, Chad Michael Snavely, Anahita Maleki, Stu Iversson, Valerie Biberaj, Nisha Moodley, Joshy Dorey, Matty Dorey, Twyla Hayes, Michael Radparvar, David Radparvar, Antonio Neves, Alexia Pinchbeck, Vicki Rox, Sarah Peck, Ash Ambirge, James Wu, Mailande Moran, Masha Maltsava, Dev Aujla, John-Michael Parker, Kym Pham, Phoebe Lapine, Jade Tailor, Marissa Andrada, Matthew Trinetti, Stacy London, Shauna Mei, Deepak Chopra, Lewis Howes, Adam Robinson, Bryony Cole, Shiva Kermani, Miki Agrawal, Radha Agrawal, and Eli Clark-Davis.

To the women in the world who inspire me daily—Cheryl Strayed, Brené Brown, Julia Cameron, Byron Katie, Oprah Winfrey, Esther Perel, and Liz Gilbert.

To my Wonder community and tribe—thank you for being brave, choosing Wonder, and speaking your wild truth. I couldn't have written this book without you.

To my family—I love you dearly.

To my father—thank you for lighting a fire inside of me that no fear could extinguish.

To my momma—you've been my biggest advocate since day one. Thank you for believing in me always, and saying "Go, baby, go" to my wildest adventures and dreams.

To Farhad—you are the great love of my life. I'm honored to be walking alongside you.

The book was written in Brooklyn, New York—in my loft "Wonderland"—and in the rice paddies and jungle of Ubud, Bali. It was edited on a train from Genevé to Paris and on a plane from SFO to JFK. I completed the final manuscript among the redwood trees of California at 1440 Multiversity in room 210.

There are 1440 minutes in each day. Let's live them fully.